HMH Florida Science

FLORIDA STATEWIDE SCIENCE ASSESSMENT (FSSA) REVIEW AND PRACTICE

GRADE 6 STUDENT BOOKLET

Houghton Mifflin Harcourt™

Science Benchmark Reviews

FSSA Practice Test

Introduction

To the Student

This booklet is designed to help you prepare to take the Florida Statewide Science Assessment (FSSA). The table of contents at the beginning of this book shows how the book is organized. The first section of the book contains review material and practice questions that are grouped by topic. Following the review material and practice questions is a practice test. The practice test is followed by an answer sheet for recording your answers for the test.

When you take the FSSA, you will be tested on the designated Science Benchmarks. Each of the Benchmarks that you may be tested on is included in the review and practice section. Reading the short review of each concept, and then answering the practice questions that follow, will be a good way to check your understanding of the material.

Taking the practice test will also help you prepare for the FSSA. The practice test should be similar to the FSSA test that you will take. After taking the practice test, you may find that there are concepts you need to review further.

Test Taking Tips

General Tips

- Read the directions carefully before you begin.

- Budget your time based on the number and type of questions. Set aside time to recheck your answers after you're done.

- When using a separate answer sheet, use a ruler or blank sheet of paper as a guide to avoid marking answers on the wrong line.

- If there is no penalty for guessing, it's better to guess than to leave an answer blank.

- Guess well, not wildly. Try to eliminate one or two answer choices first.

- Read the question fully and carefully. Many students miss the correct answer because they read only part of the question, and choose an answer based on what they think the question is asking.

- In the question stem, note key terms that tell you what to look for in the answer choices: What? When? Where? What NOT? What kind? How many?

If you encounter a question about a key term or vocabulary term that is unfamiliar to you, try to break the word up into word parts. If you know what part of the word means, you may be able to eliminate some answer choices.

Using Images

Tables and Graphs

- Read the title.

- Note the units of measure.

- For tables, read row and column headings.

- For graphs, note the data points.

- For graphs, read the axes labels.

- Look for trends and patterns.

Diagrams

- Read the title and all labels.

- Do not rely on relative sizes of items to compare size. Look for a scale.

- BEFORE you look at the diagram, read the question all the way through. Look for hints in the question that will tell you what to look at in the diagram.

- AFTER reading the question, read and look through the whole diagram to understand what it illustrates, and what processes or parts are involved.

- Follow numbered steps in order or trace arrows to understand a process.

- Look at the diagram's parts and then see how they work together.

Maps

- Read the title, key, place names, and names of other map features.

- Note the scale, compass direction, and location of important features with respect to one another.

Using Reference Sheets

- Before beginning the test, look at the reference sheets to see what is included.

- During the test, when a question addresses a topic included on the reference sheet, look at the reference sheet after you read the question.

Question Types

Multiple Choice Questions

- Read the whole question and answer it on your own before you read the answer choices.

- Read all the answer choices before you choose one.

- Read each answer choice along with the question.

- Eliminate any obviously wrong choices.

- Look for words that limit your choices, such as "most" or "best" which may indicate that there are probably several correct answers, but you should look for the one that is the most important, or had the most effect.

- If two responses are opposites, one of them is likely correct.

- Answers that include words such as *sometimes* or *often* are more likely to be correct.

Multi-Step Multiple Choice Questions

- It may not immediately be clear that a question is a multi-step problem. Read through the whole question and think about what you would need to do in order to answer the question.

- Break down the problem into the steps you would need to take in order to find the answer based on the information given in the question.

- What is the relationship between the information given and the question you are asked to answer?

- What is the useful information in the question that you will need? How many steps are necessary to get from the information to the answer?

- Outline the steps on scratch paper. Then work through each step as needed on the scratch paper. Find your answer before going back to the answer choices with the problem.

- What is the main topic of the problem? Have you answered problems on that topic before? If so, what strategies worked for you?

Formulas

$$\text{Density} = \frac{\text{mass}}{\text{volume}} \qquad\qquad D = \frac{m}{V}$$

$$\text{Average speed} = \frac{\text{total distance}}{\text{total time}} \qquad\qquad s = \frac{d}{t}$$

$$\text{Net force} = (\text{mass})(\text{acceleration}) \qquad\qquad F = ma$$

$$\text{Work} = (\text{force})(\text{distance}) \qquad\qquad W = Fd$$

Periodic Table

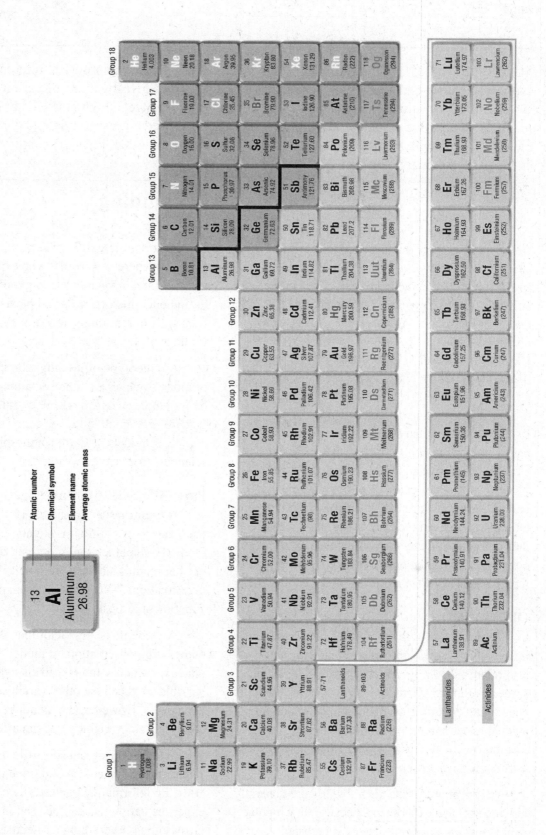

Name _____ Date _____

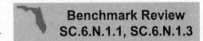

SC.6.N.1.1 Define a problem from the sixth grade curriculum: use appropriate reference materials to support scientific understanding; plan and carry out scientific investigations of various types, such as systematic observations or experiments; identify variables; collect and organize data; interpret data in charts, tables, and graphics; analyze information; make predictions; and defend conclusions.
SC.6.N.1.3 Explain the difference between an experiment and other types of scientific investigation, and explain the relative benefits and limitations of each.

Scientific Understanding

Scientists carry out investigations to learn about the natural world—everything from the smallest particles to the largest structures in the universe. The two main types of scientific investigations are *experiments* and *observations*.

Experiments and Other Types of Investigations

An **experiment** is an organized procedure to study something under controlled conditions. Experiments are often done in a laboratory. This makes it easier to control factors that can influence a result. Other investigations, such as fieldwork, surveys, or models, compare or describe the unregulated world around us. Laboratory experiments let scientists make precise observations because they can control factors. Other investigations may not easily control factors, but they may better replicate real-world conditions.

Observation

Observation is the process of obtaining information by using the senses. The word can also refer to the *information* obtained by using the senses. Although scientists make observations while conducting experiments, many things cannot be studied under controlled conditions. For example, it is impossible to create or manipulate a star. But astronomers can observe stars through telescopes.

Observations of the natural world are generally less precise than experiments because they involve factors that are not controlled by scientists. However, they may give a better description of what is actually happening in nature.

Important scientific observations can be made anywhere. A scientist who experiments with fish and oxygen levels might observe a lake to find out which animals and plants live in it. The scientist's observations may or may not support the findings of the laboratory experiment.

Another type of investigation is the creation of models, which are representations of an object or system. Models are useful for studying things that are very small, large, or complex. For example, computer models of Earth's atmosphere can help scientists forecast the weather.

Parts of a Scientific Investigation

A **hypothesis** is a testable idea or explanation that leads to scientific investigation. A scientist may think of a hypothesis after making observations or after reading findings from other scientists' investigations. The hypothesis can be tested by experiment or observation.

A **variable** is any factor that can change in an experiment, observation, or model. When scientists plan experiments, they try to change only one variable and keep the other variables constant, or unchanged. However, it may not be possible to control all the variables that can affect the results.

When carrying out scientific investigations, scientists need to collect and organize the data. **Data** are information gathered by observation or experimentation that can be used in calculating or reasoning. Everything a scientist observes in an investigation must be recorded. The setup and procedure of an experiment also need to be recorded. By carefully recording this information, scientists make sure that they will not forget important details.

Scientific Methods

Scientific methods are the ways in which scientists answer questions and solve problems. There is no single formula for an investigation. Scientists do not all use the same steps in every investigation or use steps in the same order. They may even repeat some of the steps. The following steps show one path a scientist might follow when conducting an experiment.

Defining a Problem: After making observations or reading scientific reports, a scientist might be curious about some unexplained aspect of a topic. A scientific problem is a specific question that a scientist wants to answer. The problem must be well-defined, or precisely stated, so that it can be investigated.

Forming a Hypothesis and Making Predictions: When scientists form a hypothesis, they are making an educated guess about a problem. A hypothesis must be tested to see if it is true. Before testing a hypothesis, scientists often make predictions about what will happen in an investigation.

Planning an Investigation: A scientific investigation must be carefully planned so that it tests a hypothesis in a meaningful way. Scientists need to decide whether an investigation should be done in the field or in a laboratory. They must also determine what equipment and technology are required and how materials for the investigation will be obtained.

Identifying Variables: Before conducting a controlled experiment, scientists identify all the variables that can affect the results. Then they decide which variable should change and which ones should stay constant. Some variables may be impossible to control.

Collecting and Organizing Data: The data collected in an investigation must be recorded and properly organized so that they can be analyzed. Data such as measurements and numbers are often organized into tables, charts, spreadsheets, or graphs.

A bar graph is a visual display of data that shows relationships between the data.

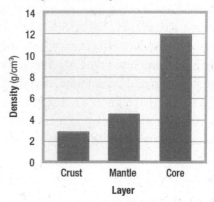

Density of Earth's Layers

A table can be used to record and organize data as it is being collected.

Density of Earth's Layers	
Layer	Density (g/cm^3)
crust	2.7– 3.3
mantle	3.3– 5.7
core	9.9– 13.1

Interpreting Data and Analyzing Information: After they finish collecting data, scientists must analyze this information. Their analysis will help them draw conclusions about the results. Scientists may have different interpretations of the same data because they analyze it using different methods.

Defending Conclusions: Scientists conclude whether the results of their investigation support the hypothesis. If the hypothesis is not supported, scientists may think about the problem some more and try to come up with a new hypothesis to test. When they publish the results of their investigation, scientists must be prepared to defend their conclusions if they are challenged by other scientists. Keep in mind that there is no single method for answering a question, nor is there one correct order of events.

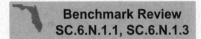

**Different Situations Require
Different Methods**

After forming a hypothesis, scientists decide how they will test it. Some hypotheses can be tested only through observation. Others must be tested in laboratory experiments. However, observation and experiments are often used together to build scientific knowledge. For example, if you want to test the strength of a metal used in airplane construction, you may study it in a laboratory experiment. But after conducting the experiment, you may want to inspect airplanes that have flown for a period of time to see how the metal holds up under actual flight conditions.

If an investigation does not support a hypothesis, it is still useful. The data from the investigation can help scientists form a better hypothesis. Scientists may go through many cycles of testing and data analysis before they arrive at a hypothesis that is supported.

Student-Response Activity

❶ Explain the difference between scientific investigations and scientific knowledge.

_____

_____

_____

❷ Explain why there is **not** one scientific method.

_____

_____

_____

❸ How are observations and hypotheses related?

_____

_____

_____

Name _____ Date _____

Read the scenario and look at the data in the graph. Then answer Questions 4–6.

The graph is taken from a study on climate change over a 100-year span.

Variation in Average Global Land Temperatures

❹ Identify a pattern that you can observe in the graph.

_____

_____

_____

_____

❺ Write a conclusion based on the data in the graph.

_____

_____

_____

_____

_____

❻ Based on the data in the graph, what might a scientist predict about the global land temperature in the future?

_____

_____

_____

_____

_____

Benchmark Assessment SC.6.N.1.1, SC.6.N.1.3

Fill in the letter of the best choice.

1 Which can be studied as a scientific investigation?

(A) Blue is the best color.

(B) Vegetarianism is better for the environment than non-vegetarianism.

(C) Country music is more enjoyable than hip-hop music.

(D) All students should be required to wear uniforms to school.

2 Which **best** describes an experiment?

(F) In a lab a scientist measures the height of roses that received different fertilizers.

(G) A scientist measures the speed at which a cheetah travels while it is hunting.

(H) A scientist measures the rate at which a population of wild geese reproduces.

(I) A scientist measures the width of a certain type of maple leaf throughout a forest.

3 Which statement about experiments is **true**?

(A) Every scientific investigation is an experiment.

(B) Scientists need fancy instruments to do experiments.

(C) Experiments do not need to be repeated in order for them to be scientifically accepted.

(D) An experiment is an organized procedure to study something under controlled conditions.

4 Look at the pie graph.

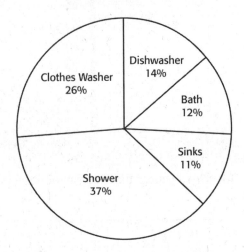

Hot Water Usage
(Based on national averages)

Based on the graph, which is a valid conclusion about hot water usage?

(F) People need to recycle more of the hot water they use.

(G) Most hot water is used by people, not by appliances.

(H) People should take fewer baths and more showers.

(I) Washing clothes by hand would save about one-fourth of the hot water people use.

5 Which must be tested to see if it is supported?

(A) a problem

(B) a variable

(C) a hypothesis

(D) a data collection

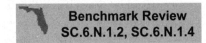

SC.6.N.1.2 Explain why scientific investigations should be replicable. **SC.6.N.1.4** Discuss, compare, and negotiate methods used, results obtained, and explanations among groups of students conducting the same investigation.

Scientific Investigations

How a Scientific Investigation Is Supported

Once a scientist performs an investigation, he or she reaches a conclusion about whether or not the results supported the hypothesis. Suppose the hypothesis is supported. What should the scientist do next? The temptation may be to announce the results to the scientific community, but it would be much too soon. The results of one single investigation are not enough evidence to consider the hypothesis valid.

Replication of a Scientific Investigation

To confirm the results of an investigation, another scientist must conduct the same experiment and get the same results. The reproduction of a scientific investigation by another person to ensure accuracy is known as *replication*. Think about an example of baking cookies. Imagine that you were able to repeat your cookie recipe with the same results three different times. You decide to give the cookie recipe to a friend. Unfortunately, your friend's batch does not taste quite as good. Your friend was not able to replicate the results. It might be that your friend did not follow the recipe exactly as you had, or maybe your friend's oven was slightly hotter than yours. Whatever the reason, you cannot confirm that the recipe is a good one until someone else uses it to produce the same delicious cookies.

Scientists must carefully describe the procedure so that anyone can follow it. Before results can be considered valid, many different scientists must be able to repeat the investigation and replicate the results. The scientists do not have to work together, or work in the same place. As long as they have a procedure, they should be able to repeat the investigation. If a study cannot be supported by the results of similar investigations, the scientific community will not accept it.

Failure to Replicate

If George, another laboratory scientist, tries to replicate an investigation of his peers, he needs to repeat the procedure in exactly the same way as in the original experiment. That includes using the same materials and setup. If George does everything the same way and gets the same results, it suggests that the results are valid. Of course, it would take many repetitions to reach such a conclusion, but this is a good start.

If George repeats the investigation but gets different results, he will need to figure out why. It could be because either he or his peer made an error or changed some aspect of the investigation. Or it could be because the original conclusion was not valid. That is why it is important for scientists to repeat investigations.

In 2015, an article in a German newspaper explained a study that found chocolate increased weight loss and helped people slim down faster. Millions of people believed that the study done by a team of scientific researchers was true, but upon further investigation and attempted replication of the study, it turned out to be false.

Name _____ Date _____

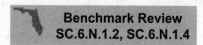

Student-Response Activity

1 Why is it important for scientists to share information from their investigations?

_____

_____

_____

_____

2 Why might a scientist repeat an investigation and not get the same results?

_____

_____

_____

_____

3 Natalie and Juan want to use an experiment that has not been replicated as the basis for their own experiment. Why might this be a bad idea?

_____

_____

_____

_____

4 Describe a time you have done or read about an experiment that has been replicated and produced different results. Explain why the results were different.

_____

_____

_____

_____

Benchmark Assessment SC.6.N.1.2, SC.6.N.1.4

Fill in the letter of the best choice.

1 What would a scientist need to replicate another scientist's experiment?

(A) only the results of the previous experiment

(B) part of the methods and procedure

(C) the methods, procedure, and results of the experiment

(D) the scientist does not need any information from the previous experiment

2 Angelica is conducting an investigation with the following procedure.

Step 1: Roll a wooden ball down a 3-meter long ramp.

Step 2: With a partner, measure the time it took for the ball to reach the bottom of the ramp.

Step 3: Roll the ball 5 more times from the same starting point of the ramp.

Step 4: Find the average time it took for the ball to reach the bottom.

Step 5: Trade procedures with another group and conduct the first 4 steps.

Which step of the procedure indicates replication?

(F) Step 1

(G) Step 2

(H) Step 3

(I) Step 5

3 Which statement provides evidence that the student replicated a peer's scientific investigation correctly?

(A) Holly decided to use a different material in her investigation than her peer used.

(B) Michael skipped one of the procedural steps, but he got similar results as his peer.

(C) Penny tested the same scientific concept as her peer, but she used a new procedure.

(D) Tony followed the exact steps of his peer's investigation.

4 Which is **true** about replication of a scientific investigation?

(F) Exact accuracy of results when replicating is not important.

(G) Results are considered valid when many different scientists repeat the results.

(H) Results are considered valid when one scientist can replicate it.

(I) Scientists need to work in the same place when replicating an investigation.

5 Which can happen if an investigation is **not** replicated?

(A) A scientist will not get recognition for his or her work.

(B) Flawed or faulty procedures in investigations do not get exposed.

(C) Scientists are confident in the results.

(D) Scientists will most likely use this investigation as evidence in future experiments.

Name _____ Date _____

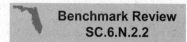

SC.6.N.2.2 Explain that scientific knowledge is durable because it is open to change as new evidence or interpretations are encountered.

Scientific Knowledge

Scientific Knowledge

Scientific knowledge gives us the most reliable methods of understanding nature. Scientific knowledge and discoveries have lasting effects on humanity and the world. Science is reliable and long lasting because of the ways in which it is developed. Being reliable and long lasting, however, does not mean that scientific knowledge does not change. In fact, part of what makes knowledge scientific is its ability to change in light of new information. An idea is only considered a scientific one if it can be tested and supported by evidence. Scientists' ideas are often called into question by new discoveries and data. Scientists then explore the questions the new discoveries raise. If the answers to the new questions do not support the idea, then the idea has to change.

History shows that new scientific ideas take time to develop into theories or to become accepted as facts or laws. Scientists should be open to new ideas, but they should always test those ideas with scientific methods. If new evidence contradicts an accepted idea, scientists must be willing to re-examine the evidence and re-evaluate their reasoning. The process of building scientific knowledge never ends. In this way, the scientific ideas that people investigate today are extensions of ideas that people have been investigating for hundreds, or even thousands, of years.

Changes in Theories

Good scientific knowledge does not always last forever. Theories and models often change with new evidence. Thus, the best scientific theories and models are those that are able to adapt to explain new observations. The theory of light is an interesting example of how scientific knowledge can adapt and change. Scientists debated the theory of light for some time. At one time, scientists saw light as particles, and later they saw it as waves. The wave theory, however, seemed to explain more about light.

For a long time, scientists accepted it.

Today, however, scientists view light as having both a particle nature and a wave nature. In a sense, the particle theory of light did not die. It was good scientific knowledge. It was just incomplete. Most scientists today would probably agree that all scientific knowledge is incomplete. Even the best theories do not explain everything. Indeed, this is the reason science continues. The goal of science is best described as the attempt to explain as much as possible and to be open to change as new evidence arises. As you study science, perhaps the best advice to remember is that everything we know about the world is simply the best guess we have made. The best scientists are those who are open to change.

Refraction in the particle theory of light	**Reflection in the wave theory of light**

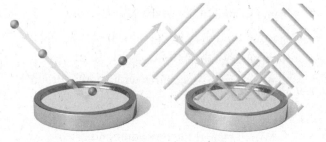

Interpretations Change Thought

Scientific knowledge about astronomy is another good example of how scientific thought changes over time. Almost everything that the earliest astronomers knew about the universe came from what they could discover with their eyes and minds. The Greek philosopher Ptolemy thought that Earth was at the center of the universe and that the other planets and the sun revolved around Earth. Then, in 1543, Copernicus published a theory that the sun was at the center of the universe and that all of the planets—including Earth—orbit the sun. He based his theory on observations he made of the movement of the planets. In 1609, an astronomer named Johannes Kepler proposed that all of the planets revolve around the sun in elliptical orbits and that the sun is not in the exact center of the orbits. Data he collected about the positions of the planets at different times supported his argument. In 1687, Isaac Newton showed that all objects in the universe attract each other through gravitational force and explained why all of the planets orbit the most massive object in the solar system—the sun. By using the work of Kepler and others, Newton was able to develop a very accurate model of the solar system.

Combined Evidence Helps Form Ideas

Isaac Newton made many contributions to multiple fields of mathematics and science. His ideas about gravity, for example, helped to shape scientific thought for hundreds of years. Newton's law of gravitation states that all matter in the universe exerts an attractive force on all the other matter in the universe. It also states that the strength of that force depends on the masses of the objects, which are attracting each other, and on the distance between them. In 1798, more than one hundred years after Newton first described the law of gravitation,

a scientist named Henry Cavendish accurately measured the gravitational constant. Newton's ideas and the evidence gathered by Cavendish enabled people to accurately predict the motion of objects in our solar system.

Newton's law of gravitation stood exactly as he first described it in 1687 until the twentieth century. Then, in 1915, Albert Einstein published his theory of general relativity. Einstein showed that gravitation depended not only on mass and distance, but on time as well. Einstein also realized that gravity is caused by the distortion of space and time. Newton had been thinking in three dimensions; Einstein introduced the fourth. By examining all of the evidence, reasoning logically, being open to change, and using creativity, Einstein was able to come up with a new and improved explanation of how the universe works. Einstein's ideas have allowed scientists to make much more precise and accurate calculations when studying extremely massive objects.

Student-Response Activity

❶ What are two scientific ideas that have changed throughout time? Explain why the ideas changed.

_____

_____

_____

_____

_____

_____

_____

_____

Name ______________________________ Date __________

Benchmark Review
SC.6.N.2.2

❷ Long ago, people thought that lightning never struck the same place twice. Over time, our understanding of weather events has changed a lot. Give at least two reasons why our understanding of lightning might have changed so much.

❸ Maria thinks that scientific knowledge never changes. Explain why Maria is incorrect and why it would be negative if scientific knowledge never changed.

❹ Why does good scientific knowledge not last forever?

Benchmark Assessment SC.6.N.2.2

Fill in the letter of the best choice.

1 Which **most likely** allowed Einstein's theory of general relativity to be an accepted piece of scientific knowledge?

(A) He had a greater level of education than Newton.

(B) He had an ability to examine evidence and be open to change.

(C) He was not open to change or new interpretations.

(D) His idea was more complex than previous ideas.

2 Which is **true** about scientific knowledge?

(F) It can never be disproven.

(G) It is often complete.

(H) It is often incomplete.

(I) It is never debated.

3 Which is the **least important** factor in deciding whether an idea is a valid scientific idea?

(A) data from observations or experiments

(B) if it can be repeated

(C) if it is able to be replicated

(D) the length of time that an idea has been around

4 In the 1800s, some scientists believed in the "rainfall follows the plow" idea, which was that breaking prairie sod would allow rainfall to be absorbed into the soil and this moisture would evaporate, causing an increase in rainfall. Which would **most likely** lead to this scientific idea being disproven and revised?

(F) a few people not believing in the idea any longer

(G) documentation of heavy rainfall in the 1800s in prairies

(H) severe droughts and improved climate data in the 1800s

(I) taller crops being grown in the 1800s than in the 1700s

5 What is the **longest** amount of time scientists might investigate a scientific idea?

(A) a couple of years

(B) a few days

(C) fourteen hours

(D) hundreds or thousands of years

SC.6.N.3.1 Recognize and explain that a scientific theory is a well-supported and widely accepted explanation of nature and is not simply a claim posed by an individual. Thus, the use of the term theory in science is very different than how it is used in everyday life.

Scientific Theories

Importance of Theories

Scientific knowledge is gathered piece by piece. Any given experiment or observation is likely to give only a small amount of data. Explanations of how the universe works, though, require thousands of points of data. In everyday usage, the word *theory* typically means an opinion or hypothesis. In science, a theory is a scientific explanation for a naturally occurring event, which is supported by a large body of evidence. Theories are used to explain a wide range of observations. A scientific theory is something that we can be very confident in. An idea must be tested many times and must be supported by evidence to be an accepted theory.

Although they are based on lots of evidence and are widely accepted, theories are subject to change and improvement. Theories are continuously investigated with new questions and subjected to testing against new evidence. Scientists recognize that theories are incomplete.

There are also some areas of knowledge in science that are referred to as laws. Laws in science are typically smaller in scope than theories in terms of what they can explain. They are scientific principles that work without exception to predict or explain nature under specific conditions. Laws are typically statements, which can be written as mathematical equations. The law of conservation of energy states that energy in a system can neither be created nor destroyed. This is fairly easy to understand conceptually. It can also be expressed mathematically.

The Scientific Theory of Plate Tectonics

One scientific theory is the theory of plate tectonics. When we look at our planet, we can only generally see the surface. We can observe many features of that surface, such as mountains, volcanoes, or deep ocean basins. For most of human history, people devised mythical stories to explain how these landforms came to be. Scientists investigated the questions that people had and collected evidence to help answer them. What scientists discovered is that large sections of Earth's surface move as units. These are called plates. Florida is part of the North American plate. Along the Pacific coast of the United States, there are many tall mountains, and even some volcanoes. These are the result of the North American and Pacific plates colliding. The theory of plate tectonics changed the study of Earth science greatly. Scientists found it could explain many things about the forces that shape Earth's surface. They observed that most major earthquakes occur close to where plates meet and press against each other. Even though we cannot observe the plates directly, the theory of plate tectonics allows us to explain many features that we can observe.

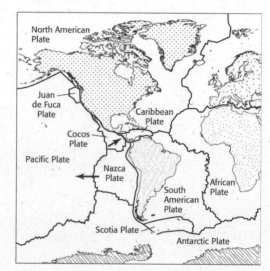

The Theory of Evolution

The scientific theory of evolution is another example of a theory. Scientists continue to improve the theory of evolution as new information is discovered. Evolution is the process by which inherited characteristics within a population change over generations, sometimes giving rise to new species. When Charles Darwin first wrote about evolution by natural selection, he did not know about the laws of inheritance or the molecular basis of traits. As scientists have learned more about these two fields of study, they have improved upon Darwin's explanation for how species change over time.

Much of the strongest evidence supporting the scientific theory of evolution comes from the fossil record. As paleontologists have uncovered more fossils over time, a more complete set of data has become available to evolutionary biologists. This has allowed scientists to revise the theory of evolution. Nearly all scientists agree that the theory of evolution accurately explains how new species have appeared on Earth over time.

Fossil Evidence of Evolution of Whales

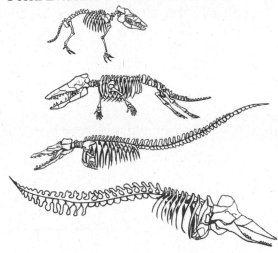

Fossil evidence of the first whales showed they were land animals with large carnivorous teeth, but their skulls resembled modern whales. As further generations went on, fossil evidence showed whales with shorter legs and hands and feet becoming enlarged and resembling paddles. More recent whales that evolved had higher levels of saltwater oxygen isotopes in their bones, showing they lived near marine habitats and were able to drink salt water as today's whales can.

Student-Response Activity

❶ What is the difference between an everyday theory and a scientific theory?

_____

_____

_____

_____

_____

_____

_____

Name ______________________ Date __________

Benchmark Review
SC.6.N.3.1

2. Both theories and laws can be used to predict what will happen in a situation that has not already been tested. Do you agree or disagree with this statement? Explain your answer.

3. Identify one theory you know of and explain why it is correctly categorized as a theory and not just a claim.

4. Francis says it is a theory that it only rains on the weekend. Explain why Francis is incorrect and that his statement is simply a claim.

Benchmark Assessment SC.6.N.3.1

Fill in the letter of the best choice.

1 Which statement is **true** about scientific theories?

- Ⓐ Any hunch you have is as good as a scientific theory.
- Ⓑ Scientific theories are widely accepted.
- Ⓒ Scientific theories cannot change when new evidence is found.
- Ⓓ We cannot be confident in scientific theories.

2 Which is the **least likely** explanation for why scientists accept the theory of plate tectonics as a valid scientific theory?

- Ⓕ Scientists observe the movement of Earth's surface and use it as evidence.
- Ⓖ Scientists can use the theory to explain many things about the forces that shape Earth's surface.
- Ⓗ Scientists widely accept this theory.
- Ⓘ A couple scientists believe it and tested it once.

3 Which statement **best** describes how an idea can become a theory?

- Ⓐ An idea is already a theory.
- Ⓑ An idea must be accepted by at least one person.
- Ⓒ An idea must be tested many times and supported by evidence.
- Ⓓ An idea must be present for at least fifty years to become a theory.

4 Which is **not** a valid scientific theory or law?

- Ⓕ the law that energy in a system can neither be created nor destroyed
- Ⓖ the theory of accumulative change in the characteristics of organisms or populations over time from generation to generation
- Ⓗ the theory that organisms such as birds can come to be from nonliving objects
- Ⓘ the theory that Earth's outer layer is divided into plates that move around

5 Which statement **best** explains why scientists accept the theory of evolution as a valid scientific theory?

- Ⓐ Scientists are able to explain how new species appeared over time by applying the theory.
- Ⓑ Scientists believe what is agreed upon by the majority of other scientists.
- Ⓒ Scientists have found an example of how the theory of evolution is true.
- Ⓓ Scientists think Charles Darwin was the smartest scientist ever.

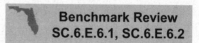
SC.6.E.6.1 Describe and give examples of ways in which Earth's surface is built up and torn down by physical and chemical weathering, erosion, and deposition. **SC.6.E.6.2** Recognize that there are a variety of different landforms on Earth's surface, such as coastlines, dunes, rivers, mountains, glaciers, deltas, and lakes, and relate these landforms as they apply to Florida.

Changes to Earth's Surface

Weathering, Erosion, and Deposition

Earth's surface is constantly changing. The processes of weathering, erosion, and deposition play a major role in building up and wearing down Earth's surface. Over time, these processes can dramatically change the appearance of Earth. Many of the landforms you see on Earth were formed or shaped by weathering, erosion, and/or deposition.

Chemical and Physical Weathering

The process by which rocks and other surfaces are broken down is called **weathering**. There are two kinds of weathering: physical and chemical.

Rocks can get smaller and smaller without a change in the composition of the rock. This is an example of a physical change. The process by which rock is broken down into smaller pieces by physical changes is **physical weathering**. Temperature changes, pressure changes, plant and animal actions, water, wind, and gravity are all agents of physical weathering. For example, when prairie dogs dig holes in the ground, they move soil to new locations. The animal's claws may scratch rocks as it digs. When the soil is moved, rocks located under the ground can be exposed. Since the rocks are now exposed to other agents of weathering such as wind and water, they are more likely to undergo weathering.

Chemical weathering involves the breakdown of rocks through chemical reactions. When these reactions occur, the composition of the rock completely changes. These changes are often accompanied by changes in color that signal that a chemical reaction has taken place.

Oxygen in the air or in water can cause chemical weathering. Oxygen reacts with the compounds that make up rock, causing chemical reactions. The process by which other chemicals combine with oxygen is called **oxidation**. Iron in rocks and soils combines quickly with oxygen that is dissolved in water. The result is a rock that turns reddish orange.

Acids break down most minerals faster than water alone. Increased amounts of acid from various sources can cause chemical weathering of rock. Acids in the atmosphere are created when chemicals combine with water in the air. When these acids fall to Earth, they are called **acid precipitation**.

Erosion and Deposition

Acting as liquid conveyor belts, rivers and streams erode soil, rock, and sediment. Sediment is tiny grains of broken-down rock. **Erosion** is the process by which sediment and other materials are moved from one place to another. Eroded materials in streams may come from the stream's own bed and banks or from materials carried to the stream by rainwater runoff. Over time, erosion causes streams to widen and deepen.

After streams erode rock and soil, they eventually drop, or deposit, their load downstream. **Deposition** is the process by which eroded material is dropped. Deposition occurs when gravity's downward pull on sediment is greater than the push of flowing water or wind. This usually happens when the water or wind slows down. A stream deposits materials along its bed, banks, and mouth, which can form different landforms.

Changing Landforms

Weathering, erosion, and deposition can result in the formation of various landforms. When water flows through streams and rivers, it erodes rock and sediment in the surrounding area. As this water cuts through rock, canyons and valleys are formed. For example, millions of years ago, the Grand Canyon was formed by the erosion of rock by the Colorado River. While some changes to Earth's surface happen quickly, most take a very long time to occur. The processes that formed the Grand Canyon happened gradually over millions of years.

There are many other landforms formed by the processes of weathering, erosion, and deposition. Floodplains, deltas, and beaches are formed as a result of deposition. The Apalachicola River, for example, carries sediments from Alabama and Georgia to Florida. Over time, this process formed the St. George barrier island.

Landforms in Florida

There are a variety of typical landforms in Florida such as coastlines, dunes, rivers, deltas, and lakes. There are also landforms such as mountains and glaciers, which have helped build up the land that is Florida today.

A **mountain** is a region of increased elevation on Earth's surface that rises to a peak. One way a mountain can form is when the collision of tectonic plates causes the Earth's crust to uplift, or rise. Another way mountains form is through the eruption of volcanoes. The highest point in Florida is Britton Hill near the Alabama border, which is 105 m in elevation. Mountains typically have an elevation of at least 300 m, meaning Florida does not have mountains! However, sediment from the Appalachian Mountains is continually being transported to areas including Florida.

A **glacier** is a mass of gradually moving or flowing ice. As snow and ice build on a mountain, the glacier can begin to move down the mountain. Glaciers scrape and relocate rocks as they move, forming sediments, and can be found at high elevations and near Earth's poles. Approximately 18,000 years ago, during a glacial period, the sea level on Earth was reduced as the water was stored in the ice. As a result, the land area of Florida was much larger than it is today. Once the ice sheet began to melt, sediments were deposited throughout the United States. In addition, the sea level rose again, altering Florida's shape and size.

Florida has approximately 30,000 lakes of varying size. A **lake** is a body of fresh or salt water that is surrounded by land. Lakes are fed by streams and rivers that carry water and sediment. The largest lake in Florida is Lake Okeechobee. A **river** is a large, natural stream of water that flows into an ocean or other large body of water, such as a lake. In Florida, most of the rivers are relatively short and do

not flow quickly because of the flat elevation of the state. Examples of Florida rivers include the St. Johns, the Apalachicola, the Suwannee, and the Peace.

When a river reaches a lake, ocean, or other body of water, the sediments carried in the river can form a delta. A **delta** is a deposit, formed by sediment, which accumulates at the mouth of a river. These landforms are often triangular in shape. Most of Florida's rivers carry a limited amount of sediment and do not flow very fast. Therefore, Florida rivers do not form large or significant deltas. An exception to this is the Apalachicola River in the Florida Panhandle.

Florida has a long coastline. A **coastline** is a dynamic boundary between land and the ocean. Coastlines can vary from rocky coasts with high, sharp cliffs, to gently sloping sandy beaches. On the western coast of Florida, the coastline forms where the land meets the Gulf of Mexico. On the eastern coast, Florida meets the Atlantic Ocean.

Sand does not easily stay in one location because of the small size of sand grains. Mounds of sand often form as wind carries and then deposits sand particles. A **dune** is a mound of wind-deposited sand. Dunes are found in both desert and coastal regions. In the desert, strong winds can carry sand depositing it into varying size dunes, from small hills to mountain-sized dunes. Coastal dunes form along coastlines. The shape of a beach, the sand supply, the wind direction, and the type of sand can determine the types of dunes formed. Dunes can have a variety of shapes including star-shaped, crescent, and straight dunes. In Florida, coastal dunes are fairly small and are found behind sandy beaches.

Student-Response Activity

1 How can each of the following agents change the shape of Earth's surface?

acid _____

waves _____

2 Describe one way that the animal in the picture causes physical weathering.

_____

_____

_____

_____

_____

_____

3 How can natural processes cause rock on a mountain to become part of a beach far away?

_____

_____

4 Fill in the Venn diagram to compare and contrast physical and chemical weathering.

Physical Weathering

Both

Chemical Weathering

Benchmark Assessment SC.6.E.6.1, SC.6.E.6.2

Fill in the letter of the best choice.

❶ Which can cause physical weathering of rock?

Ⓐ acid

Ⓑ oxygen

Ⓒ sun

Ⓓ wind

❷ Which is an example of chemical weathering?

Ⓕ carbonic acid dissolving limestone

Ⓖ growing plant roots cracking rocks

Ⓗ rocks being transported by a river

Ⓘ water melting, refreezing, and cracking rocks

❸ Look at the image.

What process does the image show?

Ⓐ chemical weathering

Ⓑ deposition

Ⓒ erosion

Ⓓ physical weathering

❹ While on a trip, Maria saw the landforms shown in the images.

Which processes formed the landforms shown?

Ⓕ the transport and deposition of sediment by ice

Ⓖ the transport and deposition of sediment by water

Ⓗ the transport and deposition of sediment by wind

Ⓘ the transport and deposition of sediment by gravity

❺ Sediment from mountains many miles away are now in the area known as Florida. Which is the **best** explanation as to how most of these sediments moved so far away from where the mountains are now?

Ⓐ The wind blew the sediments there.

Ⓑ The sediments were transported and deposited by streams and rivers.

Ⓒ The range of mountains used to be much farther south than it is now.

Ⓓ Rocks form smaller, easily transported sediment to the southern side of the mountains.

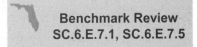
SC.6.E.7.1 Differentiate among radiation, conduction, and convection, the three mechanisms by which heat is transferred through Earth's system. **SC.6.E.7.5** Explain how energy provided by the Sun influences global patterns of atmospheric movement and the temperature differences between air, water, and land.

Heat Transfer

Heat

Heat is a type of energy that causes objects to feel hot or cold. It can be transferred between objects at different temperatures. The direction of heat transfer is always from the object with the higher temperature to the object with the lower temperature. This means that when you touch something hot, heat transfers from the object to your body.

Heat Transfer

When the same amount of energy is transferred, some materials will get warmer or cooler at a rate that is faster than other materials. Suppose you are walking on the beach on a sunny day. You may notice the land feels warmer than the air and the water, even though they are exposed to the same amount of energy from the sun. This is because the land warms up at a faster rate than the water and air do. Heat energy is transferred in three ways: radiation, convection, and conduction.

Energy Transfer by Radiation

On a summer day, you can feel warmth from the sun on your skin. How did that energy reach you from the sun? The sun transfers energy to Earth by radiation. **Radiation** is the transfer of energy as electromagnetic waves. Radiation can transfer energy between objects that are not in direct contact with each other. Many objects other than the sun also radiate energy as light and heat. These include a hot burner on a stove and a campfire.

The sun also heats land. Radiation from the sun hits land and transfers energy, causing the ground to warm. Water and air can move freely but land cannot. Even so, thermal energy stored in the ground can also be transferred. Some energy is released from the ground as radiation. Have you ever felt heat rising from the ground after a sunny day? If so, you have felt radiation.

Have you ever watched a pot of boiling water? If so, you have seen convection.

Convection is the transfer of energy due to the movement of matter. As water warms up at the bottom of the pot, some of the hot water rises. At the same time, cooler water from other parts of the pot sink and replace the rising water. This water is then warmed and the cycle continues. While convection usually happens in fluids, it can happen in solids as well. Matter—the water—has transferred heat energy due to its movement.

Convection involves the movement of matter due to differences in density. As most matter gets warmer, it undergoes thermal expansion as well as a decrease in its density. The less-dense matter gets forced upward by the surrounding colder, denser matter that sinks. As the hot matter rises, it cools and becomes denser, causing it to sink back down. This cycling of matter is called a **convection current**.

Convection takes place most often in fluids, such as water. If Earth's surface is warmer than the air, energy will be transferred from the ground to the air. As the air becomes warmer, it becomes less dense. This air is pushed upward and out of the way by cooler, denser air that is sinking. As the warm air rises, it cools and becomes denser and begins to sink back toward Earth's surface. This cycle moves energy through the atmosphere.

Convection currents also occur in the ocean because of differences in the density of ocean water. More-dense water sinks to the ocean floor, and less-dense water moves toward the surface. Temperature and the amount of salt in the water both affect the density of ocean water. Cold water is more dense than warm water, and water with a lot of salt is more dense than less-salty water.

Energy produced deep inside Earth heats rock in the mantle. The heated rock becomes less dense and is pushed up toward Earth's surface by the cooler, denser surrounding rock. Once cooled near the surface, the rock sinks. These convection currents transfer energy from Earth's core toward Earth's surface. These currents also cause the movement of tectonic plates.

Energy Transfer by Conduction

Have you ever touched an ice cube and wondered why it feels cold? An ice cube has only a small amount of energy, compared to your hand. Energy is transferred to the ice cube from your hand through the process of conduction. **Conduction** is the transfer of energy from one object to another object through direct contact. Even a solid block of ice has particles in constant motion.

Conduction involves the faster-moving particles of the warmer object transferring energy to the slower-moving particles in the cooler object. When objects of different temperatures touch, the moving particles in both objects interact. The warmer object has faster moving particles that have more kinetic energy. These particles transfer some of their energy to the object with the slower moving particles and less energy. For example, conduction happens when you place your hand on a warm object. Heat from the object warms your hand as its particles transfer energy to the particles in your hand.

Conduction allows energy to move among land, the atmosphere, and the ocean. Interactions between the ocean and the atmosphere drive global weather patterns.

Energy can be transferred between the geosphere and the atmosphere by conduction. When cooler air molecules come into direct contact with the warm ground, energy is passed to the air by conduction. Conduction between the ground and the air happens only within a few centimeters of Earth's surface.

Conduction also takes place between air particles and water particles. For example, if air transfers enough energy to liquid water, the water may evaporate. If water vapor transfers energy to the air, the kinetic energy of the water decreases. As a result, the water vapor may condense to form liquid water droplets.

Energy transfers by conduction between rock particles inside Earth. However, rock is a poor conductor of heat, so this process happens very slowly.

Wind

The next time you feel the wind blowing, you can thank the sun! The sun does not warm the whole surface of the Earth in a uniform manner. This uneven heating causes the air above Earth's surface to be at different temperatures. Cold air is more dense than warm air, which causes the cold air to sink. When the colder, more dense air sinks, it places greater pressure on the surface of Earth than warmer, less-dense air does. This results in areas of higher air pressure. Air moves from areas of higher pressure toward areas of lower pressure. The movement of air caused by differences in air pressure is called wind. The greater the differences in air pressure, the faster the air moves.

Cold, dense air at the poles causes areas of high pressure to form at the poles. Warm, less-dense air at the equator forms an area of lower pressure. This pressure gradient results in global movement of air. However, instead of moving in one circle between the equator and the poles, air moves in smaller circular patterns called **convection cells**. As air moves from the equator, it cools and becomes denser. At about 30°N latitude and 30°S latitude, a high-pressure belt results from the sinking of air. Near the poles, cold air warms as it moves away from the poles. At around 60°N latitude and 60°S latitude, a low-pressure belt forms as the warmed air is pushed upward.

Student-Response Activity

1 What is an example of conduction on Earth? Explain your answer.

_____

_____

_____

_____

2 This image shows the location of convection at different latitudes around the globe. Explain what causes convection to take place.

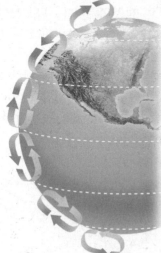

_____

_____

_____

_____

_____

_____

3 What is the main source of energy for most processes at Earth's surface?

_____

_____

4 What happens when two objects at different temperatures touch? Name one place where it occurs on Earth.

_____

_____

_____

_____

_____

Benchmark Assessment SC.6.E.7.1 and SC.6.E.7.5

Fill in the letter of the best choice.

1 When energy from the sun hits the air above land, the air warms up and rises. Along a coastline, cooler air above the ocean flows toward the land and replaces this rising air. Which **best** describes these processes?

- (A) conduction and convection
- (B) conduction, convection, and radiation
- (C) radiation and conduction
- (D) radiation and convection

2 In order for heat to transfer from one object to another, which must be **true**?

- (F) The objects must be different sizes.
- (G) The objects must be different temperatures.
- (H) The objects must be the same size.
- (I) The objects must be the same temperature.

3 Which describes what happens when cooler air particles come into contact with the warmer ground?

- (A) The particles do not interact.
- (B) Energy is transferred from the cooler air to the warmer ground.
- (C) Energy is transferred from the warmer ground to the cooler air.
- (D) The particles move back and forth between the air and the ground.

Use the image to answer Questions 4–6.

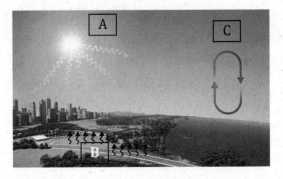

4 What takes place at Point A?

- (F) conduction
- (G) convection
- (H) radiation
- (I) sublimation

5 What takes place at Point B?

- (A) conduction
- (B) convection
- (C) radiation
- (D) sublimation

6 What takes place at Point C?

- (F) conduction
- (G) convection
- (H) radiation
- (I) sublimation

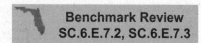
SC.6.E.7.2 Investigate and apply how the cycling of water between the atmosphere and hydrosphere has an effect on weather patterns and climate. **SC.6.E.7.3** Describe how global patterns such as the jet stream and ocean currents influence local weather in measurable terms such as temperature, air pressure, wind direction and speed, and humidity and precipitation.

The Water Cycle and Weather

Movement of Water

Movement of water among the land, oceans, atmosphere, and even living things makes up the **water cycle**. Rain, snow, and hail fall on the oceans and land because of gravity. On land, ice and water flow downhill. Water flows in streams, rivers, and waterfalls because of gravity. If the land is flat, water will collect in certain areas, forming ponds, lakes, and marshland. Some water will soak through the ground and collect underground as groundwater. Even groundwater flows downhill.

Water and snow can move upward if they turn into water vapor and rise into the air. Plants and animals also release water vapor into the air. In the air, water vapor can travel great distances with the wind. Winds can also move the water in the surface layer of the ocean by creating ocean currents. When ocean currents reach the shore or colder climates, the water will sink if it is cold enough or salty enough. The sinking water creates currents at different depths in the ocean. These are some of the ways in which water travels all over Earth.

How Does Water Reach the Atmosphere?

On Earth, water cycles through the atmosphere from the land, water, and living things. As this happens, water changes from one state to another. The changing states of water and its cycling through Earth's systems happen through the processes of evaporation, transportation, condensation, and sublimation.

Evaporation occurs when liquid water changes into water vapor. About 90% of the water in the atmosphere comes from the evaporation of Earth's water. Some water evaporates from the water on land. However, most of the water vapor evaporates from Earth's oceans. This is because oceans cover most of Earth's surface. Therefore, oceans receive most of the solar energy that reaches Earth.

Like many organisms, plants release water into the environment. Liquid water turns into water vapor inside the plant and moves into the atmosphere through stomata. Stomata are tiny holes that are found on some plant surfaces. This release of water vapor into the air by plants is called **transpiration**. About 10% of the water in the atmosphere comes from transpiration.

When solid water changes directly to water vapor without first becoming a liquid, it is called **sublimation**. This can happen when dry air blows over ice or snow, where it is very cold and the pressure is low. A small amount of the water in the atmosphere comes from sublimation.

What Happens to Water in the Atmosphere?

Water reaches the atmosphere as water vapor. In the atmosphere, water vapor mixes with other gases. To leave the atmosphere, water vapor must change into liquid or solid water. Then the liquid or solid water can fall to Earth's surface.

Condensation is the change of state from a gas to a liquid. If air that contains water vapor is cooled enough, condensation occurs. Some of the water vapor condenses on small particles, such as dust, forming little balls or tiny droplets of water. These water droplets float in the air as clouds, fog, or mist. At the ground level, water vapor may condense on cool surfaces as dew.

In clouds, water droplets may collide and "stick" together to become larger. If a droplet becomes large enough, it falls to Earth's surface as precipitation. **Precipitation** is any form of water that falls to Earth from clouds. Three common kinds of precipitation are rain, snow, and hail. Snow and hail form if the water droplets freeze. Most rain falls into the oceans because oceans cover most of Earth's surface. But winds carry clouds from the ocean over land, increasing the amount of precipitation that falls on land.

How Does the Water Cycle Affect Weather?

Weather is the short-term state of the atmosphere, including temperature, humidity, precipitation, air pressure, wind, and visibility. These elements are affected by the energy received from the sun and the amount of water in the air. To understand what influences weather, you need to understand the water cycle.

The water cycle is the continuous movement of water among the atmosphere, land, oceans, and living things. In the water cycle, water is constantly recycled among liquid, solid, and gaseous states. The water cycle involves the processes of evaporation, condensation, and precipitation.

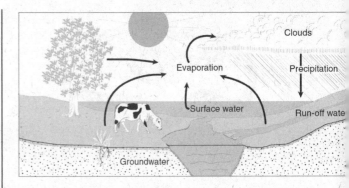

Evaporation occurs when liquid water changes into water vapor, which is a gas. Condensation occurs when water vapor cools and changes from a gas to a liquid. A change in the amount of water vapor in the air affects humidity. Clouds and fog form through condensation of water vapor, so condensation also affects visibility. Precipitation occurs when rain, snow, sleet, or hail falls from the clouds onto Earth's surface.

How Do Jet Streams Affect Weather?

Long-distance winds that travel above global winds for thousands of kilometers are called **jet streams**. Air moves in jet streams with speeds that are at least 92 kilometers per hour and are often greater than 180 kilometers per hour. Similar to global and local winds, jet streams form because Earth's surface is heated unevenly. They flow in a wavy pattern from west to east.

Each hemisphere usually has two main jet streams, a polar jet stream and a subtropical jet stream. The polar jet streams flow closer to the poles in summer than they do in winter. Jet streams can affect temperatures. For example, a polar jet stream can pull cold air down from Canada into the United States and pull warm air up toward Canada. Jet streams also affect precipitation patterns. Strong storms tend to form along jet streams. Scientists must know where a jet stream is flowing to make accurate weather predictions.

How Do Ocean Currents Influence Weather?

Global winds that blow across the surface of Earth push water across Earth's oceans, causing surface currents. Different winds cause currents to flow in different directions. The flow of surface currents moves energy as heat from one part of Earth to another. As the map below shows, both warm-water and cold-water currents flow from one ocean to another. Water near the equator carries energy from the sun to other parts of the ocean. The energy from the warm currents is transferred to colder water or to the atmosphere, changing local temperatures and humidity.

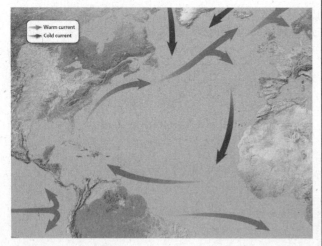

Oceans also have an effect on weather in the form of hurricanes and monsoons. Warm ocean water fuels hurricanes. Monsoons are winds that change direction with the seasons. During summer, the land becomes much warmer than the sea in some areas of the world. Moist wind flows inland, often bringing heavy rains.

How Does the Water Cycle Affect Climate?

Weather conditions change from day to day. **Climate**, on the other hand, describes the weather conditions in an area over a long period of time. For the most part, climate is determined by temperature and precipitation. The factors that affect the temperature and precipitation rates of an area include latitude, wind patterns, elevation, locations of mountains and large bodies of water, and nearness to ocean currents.

Large bodies of water, such as the ocean, can influence an area's climate. Water absorbs and releases energy as heat more slowly than land does. So, water helps moderate the temperature of nearby land. Sudden or extreme temperature changes rarely take place on land near large bodies of water.

Ocean currents can also influence an area's climate. Cold currents cool the air in coastal areas, while warm currents warm the air in coastal areas. Thus, currents moderate global temperatures. For example, the Gulf Stream is a surface current that moves warm water from the Gulf of Mexico northeastward, toward Great Britain and Europe. The British climate is mild because of the warm Gulf Stream waters. Polar bears do not wander the streets of Great Britain, as they might in Natashquan, Canada, which is at a similar latitude.

Student-Response Activity

1 Describe one way in which the water cycle impacts Earth's weather.

_____

_____

2 Fill in the Venn diagram to compare and contrast sublimation and evaporation.

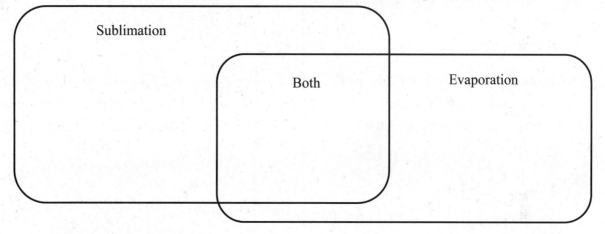

Sublimation   Both   Evaporation

Use the diagram of the water cycle to answer Questions 3 and 4.

3 Identify which process each letter represents.

A _____

B _____

C _____

D _____

E _____

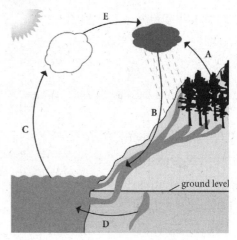

4 How do the labeled processes influence weather?

B _____

C _____

E _____

5 How does the polar jet stream affect temperature and precipitation in North America?

_____

_____

Benchmark Assessment SC.6.E.7.2, SC.6.E.7.3

Fill in the letter of the best choice.

1 Which process can result when liquid water absorbs energy?

(A) condensation

(B) evaporation

(C) freezing

(D) precipitation

Use the diagram showing the movement of water from Earth's surface into the atmosphere to answer Questions 2 and 3.

2 Which process is shown by arrow A?

(F) condensation

(G) evaporation

(H) sublimation

(I) transpiration

3 Which process is shown by arrow C?

(A) condensation

(B) evaporation

(C) sublimation

(D) transpiration

4 Which is the main energy source for the water cycle?

(F) animals

(G) coal

(H) plants

(I) sun

Use the diagram showing water returning to Earth's surface to answer Questions 5 and 6.

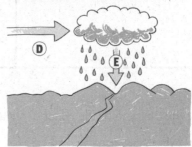

Water returns to Earth's surface.

5 Arrow D is the result of which process?

(A) water vapor in the air cools and condenses

(B) water vapor in the air cools and evaporates

(C) water droplets collide and get heavier

(D) liquid water changes to water vapor

6 Arrow E is the result of which process?

(F) water vapor in the air cools and condenses

(G) water vapor in the air cools and evaporates

(H) water droplets collide and get heavier

(I) liquid water changes to water vapor

SC.6.E.7.4 Differentiate and show interactions among the geosphere, hydrosphere, cryosphere, atmosphere, and biosphere. SC.6.E.7.6 Differentiate between weather and climate. SC.6.E.7.9 Describe how the composition and structure of the atmosphere protects life and insulates the planet.

The Atmosphere and Biosphere

What Are Earth's Systems?

A system is a group of related objects or parts that work together to form a whole. From the center of the planet to the outer edge of the atmosphere, Earth is a system. The Earth system is all of the matter, energy, and processes within Earth's boundary. Earth is a complex system made up of many smaller systems. The Earth system is made of nonliving things, such as rocks, air, and water. It also contains living things, such as trees, animals, and people.

Matter and energy continuously cycle through the smaller systems that make up the Earth system. The Earth system can be divided into five main parts—the geosphere, the hydrosphere, the cryosphere, the atmosphere, and the biosphere.

The Five Main Systems

The **geosphere** is the mostly solid, rocky part of Earth. It extends from the center of Earth to the outer layer. The core, mantle, and crust make up the geosphere. The crust is the thin, outermost layer of the geosphere. The crust is divided into plates that move slowly over Earth's surface. The crust beneath the oceans is called oceanic crust, and is only 5 to 10 km thick. The continents are made of continental crust, and they range in thickness from about 15 to 70 km. Continental crust is thickest beneath mountain ranges. The crust is made mostly of silicate minerals.

The mantle lies just below the crust. A small layer of the solid mantle, right below the crust, is just soft enough to flow. Movements in this layer move the plates of the crust. The mantle is about 2,900 km thick. It is made of silicate minerals that are denser than those in the crust.

The central part of Earth is the core, which has a radius of 3,500 km. It is made of iron and nickel and is very dense.

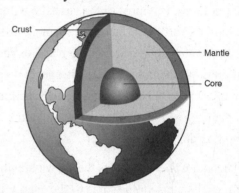

The **hydrosphere** is the part of Earth that is liquid water. Ninety-seven percent of all water on Earth is the salt water found in the oceans. Oceans cover 71% of Earth's surface. The hydrosphere also includes the water in lakes, rivers, and marshes. Clouds and rain are also parts of the hydrosphere. Even water that is underground is part of the hydrosphere. The water on Earth is constantly moving. It moves through the ocean in currents, because of wind and differences in the density of ocean waters. Water also moves from Earth's surface to the air by evaporation. It falls back to Earth as rain. It flows in rivers and through rocks under the ground. It even moves into and out of living things.

Earth's **cryosphere** is made up of all of the frozen water on Earth. Therefore, all of the snow, ice, sea ice, glaciers, ice shelves, icebergs, and frozen ground are a part of the cryosphere. Most of the frozen water on Earth is found in the ice caps in Antarctica and in the Arctic. However, snow and glaciers are found in the mountains and at high altitudes all over the world. The amount of frozen water in most of these areas often changes with the seasons. These changes, in turn, play an important role in Earth's climate and in the survival of many species.

The **atmosphere** is a mixture of mostly invisible gases that surrounds Earth. The atmosphere extends outward about 500 to 600 km from the surface of Earth. But most of the gases lie within 8 to 50 km of Earth's surface. The main gases that make up the atmosphere are nitrogen and oxygen. About 78% of the atmosphere is nitrogen. Oxygen makes up 21% of the atmosphere. The remaining 1% is made up of many other gases, including argon, carbon dioxide, and water vapor.

The atmosphere contains the air we breathe. The atmosphere also traps some of the energy from the sun's rays. This energy helps keep Earth warm enough for living things to survive and multiply. Uneven warming by the sun gives rise to winds and air currents that move large amounts of air around the world.

The atmosphere surrounds and protects Earth. It also protects Earth from harmful solar radiation and from space debris that enters the Earth system. The ozone layer is an area in the stratosphere, 15 km to 40 km above Earth's surface, where ozone is highly concentrated. The ozone layer absorbs most of the solar radiation.

The atmosphere also controls the temperature on Earth. Without the atmosphere, Earth's average temperature would be very low. The greenhouse effect is the process by which gases in the atmosphere, such as water vapor and carbon dioxide, absorb and give off infrared radiation. Radiation from the sun warms Earth's surface, and Earth's surface gives off infrared radiation.

The **biosphere** is made up of living things and the areas of Earth where they are found. The rocks, soil, oceans, lakes, rivers, and lower atmosphere all support life. Organisms have even been found deep in Earth's crust and high in clouds. But no matter where they live, all organisms need certain factors to survive. Many organisms need oxygen or carbon dioxide to carry out life processes. Liquid water is also important for most living things. Many organisms also need moderate temperatures. You will not find a polar bear living in a desert because it is too hot for the polar bear. However, some organisms do live in extreme environments, such as in ice at the poles and at volcanic vents on the sea floor. A stable source of energy is also important for life. For example, plants and algae use the energy from sunlight to make their food. Other organisms get their energy by eating these plants or algae.

Interactions Among Earth's Systems

Earth's spheres interact as matter and energy change and cycle among the five different spheres. These interactions make life on Earth possible. Remember that the Earth system includes all the matter, energy, and processes within Earth's boundary.

If matter or energy never changed from one form to another, life on Earth would not be possible. Imagine what would happen if there were no more rain and all fresh water drained into the oceans. Most of the life on land would quickly die. But how do these different spheres interact? An example of an interaction is when water cycles among land, ocean, air, and living things. To move between and among these different spheres, water absorbs, releases, and transports energy all over the world in its different forms.

Matter and Energy Exchanged Among Spheres

Earth's spheres interact as matter moves between and among spheres. For example, the atmosphere interacts with the hydrosphere or cryosphere when rain or snow falls from the air. The opposite also happens as water from the hydrosphere and cryosphere moves into the atmosphere. Sometimes, matter moves through different spheres. For example, some bacteria in the biosphere remove nitrogen gas from the atmosphere. These bacteria then release a different form of nitrogen into the soil, or geosphere. Plants in the biosphere use this nitrogen to grow. When the plant dies and decays, the nitrogen is released in different forms. One of these forms returns to the atmosphere.

Earth's spheres also interact as energy moves between them. For example, plants use solar energy to make their food. Some of this energy is passed on to animals that eat plants. Some of the energy is released into the atmosphere as heat as the animals move around. Some of the energy is released into the geosphere when organisms die and decay. In this case, energy enters the biosphere and moves into the atmosphere and geosphere.

Energy also moves back and forth between spheres. For example, solar energy reflected by Earth's surface warms up the atmosphere, creating winds. Winds create waves and surface ocean currents that travel across the world's oceans. When warm winds and ocean currents reach colder areas, thermal energy moves into the colder air, warming it up. In this case, the energy has cycled between the atmosphere and the hydrosphere.

Weather and Climate

Weather conditions change from day to day. Weather is the condition of Earth's atmosphere at a particular time and place. Climate, on the other hand, describes the weather conditions in an area over a long period of time. For the most part, climate is determined by temperature and precipitation. But what factors affect the temperature and precipitation rates of an area? Those factors include latitude, wind patterns, elevation, locations of mountains and large bodies of water, and nearness to ocean currents.

Student-Response Activity

❶ What are the five main parts of the Earth system? Provide a description for each part.

_____

_____

_____

_____

_____

2 Fill in the Venn diagram to compare the hydrosphere and the cryosphere.

Hydrosphere

Both

Cryosphere

3 What would happen to life on Earth if the ozone layer were not present?

_____

_____

_____

4 Use the diagram to list examples of things that make up the biosphere, hydrosphere, and geosphere.

_____

_____

_____

_____

Benchmark Assessment SC.6.E.7.4, SC.6.E.7.6, SC.6.E.7.9

Fill in the letter of the best choice.

For Questions 1 and 2, use the graph showing the composition of Earth's atmosphere. Each part represents a type of gas.

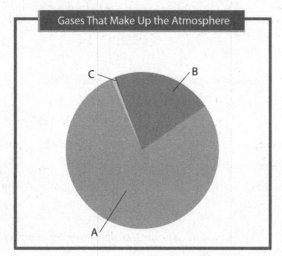

Gases That Make Up the Atmosphere

❶ Which gas is represented by part A on the graph?

Ⓐ carbon dioxide

Ⓑ nitrogen

Ⓒ oxygen

Ⓓ water vapor

❷ Which gas is represented by part B on the graph?

Ⓕ carbon dioxide

Ⓖ nitrogen

Ⓗ oxygen

Ⓘ water vapor

❸ Which is an example of the cycling of matter from one sphere to another?

Ⓐ a puddle of water evaporating and rising into the atmosphere

Ⓑ animals obtaining energy from plants

Ⓒ heat energy from the sun warming the land

Ⓓ heat energy from the sun warming the oceans

❹ When heat moves from the ocean to the surrounding air, which is this an example of?

Ⓕ the transfer of energy from the atmosphere to the hydrosphere

Ⓖ the transfer of energy from the hydrosphere to the atmosphere

Ⓗ the transfer of matter from the atmosphere to the hydrosphere

Ⓘ the transfer of matter from the hydrosphere to the atmosphere

❺ Which system includes all life on Earth?

Ⓐ biosphere

Ⓑ cryosphere

Ⓒ geosphere

Ⓓ hydrosphere

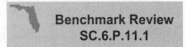
SC.6.P.11.1 Explore the Law of Conservation of Energy by differentiating between potential and kinetic energy. Identify situations where kinetic energy is transformed into potential energy and vice versa.

The Law of Conservation of Energy

Forms of Energy

Imagine that you are biking up a hill. You would use one type of energy to go up the hill. At the top, the bike gains a second type of energy you can use to go down the hill. These two types of energy are called kinetic energy and potential energy.

Kinetic energy is the energy of motion. All moving objects have kinetic energy. Like all forms of energy, kinetic energy has the ability to cause change. When a hammer moves towards a nail, it has kinetic energy. This kinetic energy can be used to move the nail into a piece of wood. A change has occurred.

The amount of kinetic energy an object has depends on two things: mass and speed. The more mass a moving object has, the more kinetic energy it has. If there are two objects moving at the same speed, then the one with more mass will have more kinetic energy. For example, if a car and a bike are both moving at the same speed, then the car will have more kinetic energy because it has more mass. Kinetic energy also depends on speed. The faster an object moves, the more kinetic energy it has. If there are two objects with the same mass, then the one going faster will have more kinetic energy. A cheetah has more kinetic energy when it is running than when it is walking.

Not all energy has to do with motion. Some energy is stored energy, or potential energy. **Potential energy** is the stored energy that an object has due to its position, condition, or chemical composition. Like kinetic energy, stored potential energy has the ability to cause

change. For example, a book held in your hands has potential energy. If you drop it, its position will change.

One type of potential energy is called gravitational potential energy. Gravity is the force that pulls objects toward Earth's center. When you lift an object, you transfer energy to the object and give the object gravitational potential energy. Any object above the ground has gravitational potential energy.

The amount of gravitational potential energy that an object has depends on its mass and its height above the ground. Gravitational potential energy increases as an object's distance from the ground, or from its lowest possible position, increases. A skydiver has more gravitational potential energy on the plane than she does after she jumps out and gets closer to the ground. Gravitational potential energy also increases as mass increases. If there are two skydivers on the plane, the one with more mass will have more gravitational potential energy.

Law of Conservation of Energy

The law of conservation of energy states that energy can be neither created nor destroyed. It can only be transformed.

As a skater rolls down a ramp, the amounts of potential and kinetic energy change. However, the law of conservation of energy requires that the total energy stays the same, assuming no energy is converted into other forms such as heat or light. In order for the total energy to remain the same, some of the potential energy changes to kinetic energy. At other times, some kinetic energy changes to potential energy. At the top of the ramp, the skater has potential energy but no kinetic energy (he is not moving). As the skater moves closer to the ground, he loses potential energy, but gains the same amount of kinetic energy. As he rolls down the ramp, his potential energy decreases because his distance from the ground decreases. His kinetic energy increases because his speed increases.

Student-Response Activity

❶ Complete the Venn diagram to compare and contrast gravitational potential energy and kinetic energy.

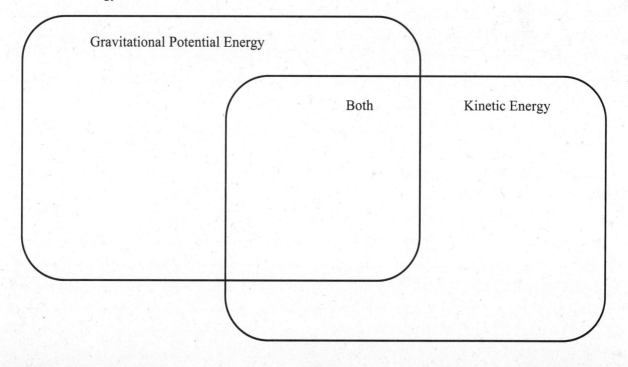

Gravitational Potential Energy

Both

Kinetic Energy

Name ______________________ Date __________

Benchmark Review
SC.6.P.11.1

❷ A tennis ball and a marble are rolling on the floor at the same speed. Which has more kinetic energy?

____

____

____

____

❸ Which has more potential energy: a book on the floor or the same book on a table? Explain your answer.

____

____

____

____

❹ How is energy conserved when a skater goes down a ramp?

____

____

____

____

____

Benchmark Assessment SC.6.P.11.1

Fill in the letter of the best choice.

1 Each vehicle below is traveling at the same speed. Which has the **most** kinetic energy?

(A) car
(B) bike
(C) bird
(D) truck

2 Which is **true** about a flying bird?

(F) The bird has only kinetic energy.
(G) The bird has only potential energy.
(H) The bird has both kinetic and potential energy.
(I) The bird has neither kinetic nor potential energy.

3 Which statement about the law of conservation of energy is **true**?

(A) Energy can be destroyed, but not created.
(B) Energy is neither created nor destroyed.
(C) The total energy changes over time.
(D) New energy can be created.

A student looks at the image of a ball rolling down a ramp. The image shows four different positions for the ball Use this image to answer Questions 4–5.

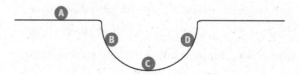

4 At which point does the ball have the **greatest** gravitational potential energy?

(F) A
(G) B
(H) C
(I) D

5 At which point does the ball have the **greatest** kinetic energy?

(A) A
(B) B
(C) C
(D) D

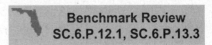
SC.6.P.12.1 Measure and graph distance versus time for an object moving at a constant speed. Interpret this relationship. **SC.6.P.13.3** Investigate and describe that an unbalanced force acting on an object changes its speed, or direction of motion, or both.

Unbalanced Forces, Motion, and Speed

Describing Location

Have you ever gotten lost while looking for a specific place? If so, you probably know that the description of the location can be very important. Suppose you are trying to describe your location to a friend. How would you explain where you are? You need two pieces of information: a position and a reference point.

With a Position

Position describes the location of an object. Often, you describe where something is by comparing its position with where you currently are. For example, you might say that a classmate sitting next to you is two desks to your right, or that a mailbox is two blocks south of where you live. Each time you identify the position of an object, you are comparing the location of the object with the location of another object or place.

With a Reference Point

When you describe a position by comparing it to the location of another object or place, you are using a reference point. A **reference point** is a location to which you compare other locations. In the mailbox example above, the reference point is "where you live." Suppose you are at a zoo with some friends. If you are using the map to the right, you could describe your destination using different reference points. Using yourself as the reference point, you might say that the red panda house is one block east and three blocks north of your current location. Or you might say the red panda

house is one block north and one block east of the fountain. In this example, the fountain is your reference point.

What Is Motion?

An object moves, or is in motion, when it changes its position relative to a reference point. **Motion** is a change in position over time. If you were to watch a girl on a bike, you would see her move. If you were not able to watch her, you might still know something about her motion. If you saw that the biker was in one place at one time and a different place later, you would know that she had moved. A change in position is evidence that motion has happened. If the biker returned to her starting point, you might not know that she had moved. The starting and ending positions cannot tell you everything about motion.

What Is Speed?

A change in an object's position tells you that motion took place, but it does not tell you how quickly the object changed position. The **speed** of an object is a measure of how far something moves in a given amount of time. In other words, speed measures how quickly or slowly the object changes position. In the same amount of time, a faster object would move farther than a slower moving object.

The speed of an object is rarely constant. For example, a biker may travel quickly when she begins a race, but may slow down as she gets tired at the end of the race. Average speed is a way to calculate the speed of an object that may not always be moving at a constant speed. Instead of describing the speed of an object at an exact moment, average speed describes the speed over a stretch of time.

Graphing Constant Speed

A convenient way to show the motion of an object is by using a graph that plots the distance the object has traveled against time. This type of graph is called a distance-time graph. You can use it to see how both distance and speed change with time.

How far away the object is from a reference point is plotted on the *y*-axis. So the *y*-axis expresses distance in units such as meters, centimeters, or kilometers. Time is plotted on the *x*-axis, and can display units such as seconds, minutes, or hours. If an object moves at a constant speed, the graph is a straight line.

You can use a distance-time graph to determine the average speed of an object. The slope, or steepness, of the line is equal to the average speed of the object. You calculate the average speed for a time interval by dividing the change in distance by the change in time for that time interval.

Suppose that a horse is running at a constant speed. The distance-time graph of its motion is shown below. To calculate the speed of the horse, choose two data points from the graph below and calculate the slope of the line. The calculation of the slope uses the change in *y* (140 m -70 m) divided by the change in *x* (10 s - 5 s). Since we know that the slope of a line on a distance-time graph is its average speed, then we know that the horse's speed is 14 m/s.

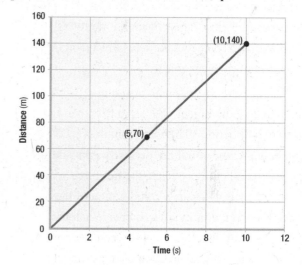

How are changing speeds graphed? Some distance-time graphs show the motion of an object with a changing speed. In these distance-time graphs, the change in the slope of a line indicates that the object has sped up, slowed down, or stopped.

As an object moves, the distance it travels increases with time. The motion can be seen as a climbing line on the graph. The slope of the line indicates speed. Steeper lines show intervals where the speed is greater than intervals with less steep lines. If the line gets steeper, the object is speeding up. If the line gets less steep, the object is slowing. If the line becomes flat, or horizontal, the object is not moving. In this interval, the speed is zero meters per second.

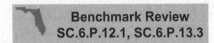
Changes in Speed or Direction

When the forces on an object produce a net force of 0 N, the forces are balanced. **Balanced forces** will not cause a change in the motion of a moving object, and they will not cause a nonmoving object to start moving. Many objects around you have only balanced forces acting on them. When the net force is not 0 N, the forces on the object are unbalanced. **Unbalanced forces** produce a change in motion, such as a change in speed or direction. This change in motion is acceleration. The acceleration is always in the direction of the net force.

When the forces on an object are unbalanced, the object will begin to move, but in which direction? The forces on an object can be unbalanced but not perfectly opposite in direction. When this occurs, the net force will be in a direction that is a combination of the directions of the individual forces. When the forces are not of equal strength, the direction will be closer to the direction of the stronger force.

Forces Act on Objects

You know that force and motion are related. When you exert a force on a football by kicking it with your foot, or throwing it in the air, the ball will change its motion. In the 1680s, Sir Isaac Newton explained this relationship between force and motion with three laws of motion. Newton's first law describes the motion of an object that has a net force of 0 N acting on it. The law states: *An object at rest remains at rest, and an object in motion maintains its velocity unless it experiences an unbalanced force.* This law is easier to understand when broken down into parts.

An object at rest remains at rest . . . unless it experiences an unbalanced force. An object that is not moving is said to be at rest. A desk in a classroom, or a football on a kicking tee, are both examples of objects at rest. Newton's

first law says that objects at rest will stay at rest unless acted on by an unbalanced force. An object will not start moving until a push or a pull is exerted upon it. So, a desk will not slide across the floor unless a force pushes the desk, and a football will not move off the tee until a force pushes, or kicks, it off. Nothing at rest starts moving until a force makes it move.

An object in motion maintains its velocity unless it experiences an unbalanced force. The second part of Newton's first law is about objects with a certain velocity. Such objects will continue to move forever with the same velocity unless an unbalanced force acts on them. Think about coming to a sudden stop while riding a bike. The bike comes to a stop when the brakes are applied. But your body feels like it is moving forward, so you must hold and push back against the handlebars forcing the motion of your body to stop with the bike. These two parts of the law are really stating the same thing. Remember that an object at rest has a velocity—its velocity is zero.

Newton's first law is also called the law of inertia. **Inertia** is the tendency of all objects to resist any change in motion. Because of inertia, an object at rest will remain at rest until a force makes it move. Likewise, inertia is why a moving object will maintain its velocity until a force changes its speed or direction. Inertia is why it is impossible for a bicycle, a car, or a train to stop immediately.

Acceleration

When an unbalanced force acts on an object, the object moves with accelerated motion. Newton's second law describes the motion: *The acceleration of an object depends on the mass of the object and the amount of force applied.* This law links force, mass, and acceleration. Suppose you are pushing a wagon. When the wagon is empty, it has less mass, so your force accelerates the wagon quickly. But when someone is sitting in the wagon, the same push accelerates the wagon more slowly.

Student-Response Activity

1 What are two pieces of information that are needed to describe the location of an object?

_____

_____

2 When two forces acting on a moving object are unbalanced, what can happen to this object?

_____

_____

3 Joe and Toby both rode their bikes to the library. They left their homes at noon and both arrived at the same time. Examine the map below that shows the location of Joe's house, Toby's house, and the library. Who traveled at the greater speed? Explain your answer.

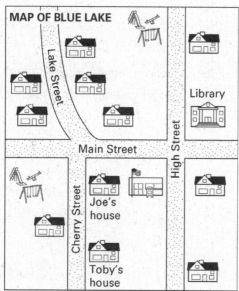

_____

_____

_____

_____

_____

_____

4 Explain the movement of the zebra in your own words.

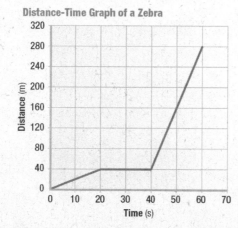

_____

_____

_____

_____

_____

Benchmark Assessment SC.6.P.12.1, SC.6.P.13.3

Fill in the letter of the best choice.

A student examines a distance-time graph of a squirrel. Use this graph to answer Questions 1–3.

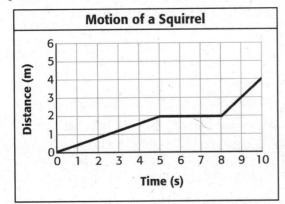

1 During which time interval is the squirrel traveling at the fastest speed?

Ⓐ 1–2 min

Ⓑ 2–3 min

Ⓒ 5–6 min

Ⓓ 8–9 min

2 At which point does the squirrel stop moving?

Ⓕ 1–2 min

Ⓖ 2–3 min

Ⓗ 5–8 min

Ⓘ 9–10 min

3 During which time interval did the squirrel travel the farthest?

Ⓐ 1–2 min

Ⓑ 3–4 min

Ⓒ 5–8 min

Ⓓ 8–10 min

4 The motion of four cars is described below. Which car has the highest speed?

Ⓕ a car that travels 10 km in 0.5 hour

Ⓖ a car that travels 15 km in 1 hour

Ⓗ a car that travels 20 km in 1 hour

Ⓘ a car that travels 30 km in 0.5 hour

5 Unbalanced forces cause a change in speed, motion, or both. Which must have an unbalanced force acting on it?

Ⓐ a stopped car

Ⓑ a ball on the floor

Ⓒ a ball rolling down a hill

Ⓓ a horse running at a constant speed

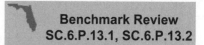
SC.6.P.13.1 Investigate and describe types of forces, including contact forces and forces acting at a distance, such as electrical, magnetic, and gravitational. **SC.6.P.13.2** Explore the Law of Gravity by recognizing that every object exerts gravitational force on every other object and that the force depends on how much mass the objects have and how far apart they are.

Types of Forces

Force

In science, a **force** is simply a push or a pull. Forces are vectors, meaning that they have both a magnitude and a direction. A force can cause an object to accelerate, and thereby change the speed or direction of motion. In fact, when you see a change in an object's motion, you can infer that one or more forces acted on the object. These forces are said to be unbalanced because they are unequal in size. When an object is not changing speed or direction in motion it means that there are balanced forces acting on it. These forces are equal in size but opposite in direction.

The unit that measures force is the newton (N). One newton is equal to one kilogram-meter per second squared ($kg \cdot m/s^2$).

All forces exist only when there is something for them to act on. However, a force can act on an object without causing a change in motion. For example, when you sit on a chair, the downward force you exert on the chair does not cause the chair to move, because the floor exerts a counteracting upward force on the chair.

How Do Forces Act?

It is not always easy to tell what is exerting a force or what is acted on by a force. Forces can be contact forces, as when one object touches or bumps into another. When you use your muscles to push on a box to move it, you exert a contact force on the box.

Another type of contact force is friction. Friction happens when one object that is moving touches another object. Friction causes some of the energy of motion to become heat energy. This energy transformation causes the object to slow down. Air resistance is a type of friction that happens when an object moves through the air.

Forces can also act at a distance. Magnetic force is an example of a force that can act at a distance. The magnet does not have to be directly touching the metal to be held to it. A magnetic force can hold a magnet to a refrigerator even when there is something in the way, such as paper or a photograph.

Electrical forces are another type of force that acts over a distance. Particles of opposite charge are pulled towards each other. Particles of the same charge are pushed away from each other. If you have ever gotten a shock when you touch a doorknob after shuffling along the carpet, you have felt an electrical force. As you move along the carpet, your shoes pick up loose electrons. Electrons have a negative charge. When you touch the metal doorknob, the electrons jump off you and onto the metal.

The Force of Gravity

When you jump up, a force called gravity pulls you back to the ground even though you are separated from Earth.

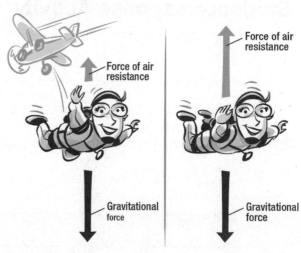

If you watch a video of astronauts on the moon, you will see them wearing big, bulky spacesuits, yet jumping lightly. Why is leaping on the moon easier than on Earth? The answer is gravity. Gravity is a force of attraction between objects due to their mass. Gravity is a noncontact force that acts between two objects at any distance apart.

The law of universal gravitation relates gravitational force, mass, and distance. It states that all objects attract each other through gravitational force. The strength of the force depends on the masses involved and distance between them.

The gravitational force between two objects increases as the distance between their centers decreases. This means that objects far apart have a weaker attraction than objects close together. If two objects move closer, the attraction between them increases. For example, you cannot feel the sun's gravity because it is so far away, but if you were able to stand on the surface of the sun, you would find it impossible to move due to the gravity!

The gravitational force between two objects increases with the mass of each object. This means that objects with greater mass have more attraction between them. A cow has more mass than a cat, so there is more attraction between the Earth and the cow, and the cow weighs more. This part of the law of universal gravitation explains why astronauts on the moon bounce when they walk. The moon has less mass than Earth, so the astronauts weigh less. The force of each step pushes an astronaut higher than it would on Earth.

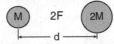

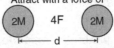

Student-Response Activity

❶ What is a force?

_____

_____

❷ What are two factors that affect the strength of gravitational force between two objects?

_____

_____

_____

_____

❸ Complete the Venn diagram to compare contact forces and forces that act over a distance.

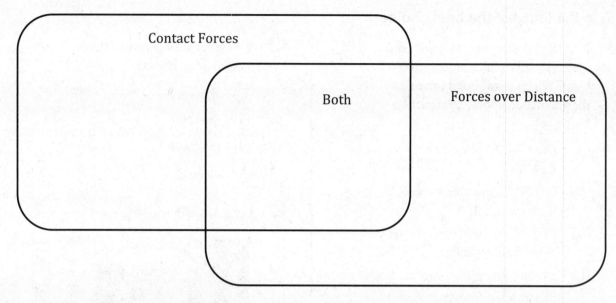

Contact Forces

Both

Forces over Distance

❹ Suzanna notices that when she rolls a marble on the carpet, the marble slows down and stops. What force causes the marble to change its motion? How does this force act?

_____

_____

_____

_____

_____

_____

_____

❺ Explain the difference between balanced and unbalanced forces.

_____

_____

_____

_____

_____

Benchmark Assessment SC.6.P.13.1, SC.6.P.13.2

Fill in the letter of the best choice.

1 A student is experimenting with two identical balls, which are 1 meter apart. Which change will increase the gravitational force of attraction the most?

(A) doubling the distance between the balls

(B) cutting the distance between the balls in half

(C) pushing the balls one centimeter closer to one another

(D) moving the balls so they are three meters apart from one another

2 Ignacio uses a hammer to hit a nail into a board on the floor. How does gravity make it easier to hammer the nail?

(F) Gravity pushes the board up to help the nail go in.

(G) Gravity pulls the board and the nail toward one another.

(H) Gravity pulls the hammer down so it pushes on the nail.

(I) Gravity pulls the nail down, but it does not pull on the hammer.

3 Which force attracts all matter together?

(A) friction
(B) gravity
(C) magnetic
(D) electrical

4 Which force slows down the motion of an object?

(F) friction
(G) gravity
(H) magnetic
(I) electrical

5 Look at the image below.

Which force holds the paper to the refrigerator?

(A) friction
(B) gravity
(C) magnetic
(D) electrical

SC.6.L.14.1 Describe and identify patterns in the hierarchical organization of organisms from atoms to molecules and cells to tissues to organs to organ systems to organisms.

Cellular Organization

The Smallest Particles

All matter in the universe, including living matter, is made from tiny particles called **atoms**. Atoms are made up of exactly one type of matter, such as hydrogen or oxygen. **Molecules** are the smallest unit of matter of a substance that retains all the physical and chemical properties of that substance. Molecules can consist of a single atom or a group of atoms bonded together. Water molecules, for example, are made up of two hydrogen atoms and one oxygen atom. Atoms and molecules are essential to all living things.

Cells

An **organism** is a living thing that can carry out life processes by itself. Unicellular organisms are made up of just one cell that performs all of the functions necessary for life. Having only one cell has advantages and disadvantages. For example, unicellular organisms need fewer resources. Some can live in harsh conditions, such as hot springs and very salty water. However, unicellular organisms are very small, which means they may be eaten by larger organisms. Another disadvantage of being unicellular is that the entire organism dies if the single cell dies.

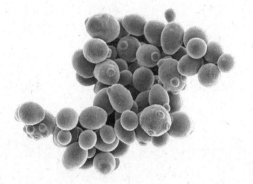

Multicellular organisms are made up of more than one cell. These cells are grouped into different levels of organization, including tissues, organs, and organ systems. The cells that make up a multicellular organism, such as humans and plants, may be specialized to perform specific functions. Different cells have different functions in the body. This specialization makes the multicellular organism more efficient. Other benefits of being multicellular are larger size and longer life span. There are disadvantages to being multicellular, too. Multicellular organisms need more resources than unicellular organisms do. Also, the cells of multicellular organisms are specialized for certain jobs, which means that cells must depend on each other to perform all of the functions that an organism needs. A multicellular organism can have four levels of organization: cells, tissues, organs, and organ systems.

Tissues

A tissue is a group of similar cells that perform a common function. Most animals are made of four basic types of tissues: nervous, epithelial, connective, and muscle. The function of nervous tissue is to pass messages around the body. Epithelial tissue protects the body by forming boundaries, such as linings of organs. Connective tissue is responsible for holding parts of the body together and for supporting and nourishing organs. Muscle tissue is responsible for movement.

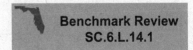
Plants are made of different types of tissues than animals. The three types of tissues that plants contain are transport, protective, and ground. Water and nutrients are moved through the plant by protective tissues. Protective tissues protect the outside of the plant. Ground tissues are responsible for supporting the plant and storage.

Organs

An **organ** is a structure made up of a collection of tissues that carries out a specialized function. The heart is an organ that pumps blood containing nutrients and oxygen around the body. Multiple types of tissues must work together for organs to function. For example, nervous tissue sends messages to muscle tissue in the heart to tell the muscle tissue to contract. When the muscle tissue contracts, the heart pumps blood throughout the body.

Plants also contain organs that require different tissue types to work together. A leaf is an organ that contains all three types of plant tissues. The leaf is able to reduce water loss because of its protective tissue. The ground tissue in the leaf is used for photosynthesis. Nutrients are distributed from the leaves to the stems by transport tissue.

Organ Systems

An **organ system** is a group of organs that work together to perform body functions. Each organ system has a specific job to do for the organism. For example, the stomach works with other organs of the digestive system to digest and absorb nutrients from food. Other organs included in the digestive system are the esophagus and the small and large intestines. The diagram below shows the organs of the digestive system.

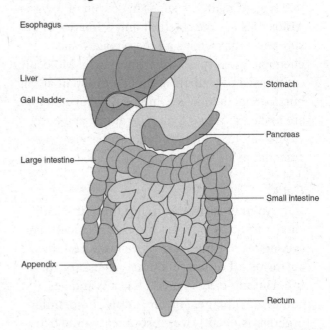

Student-Response Activity

❶ What are the levels of organization in multicellular organisms?

_____

_____

_____

_____

❷ Fill in the Venn diagram to compare the functions of animal tissues and plant tissues. What functions do they share?

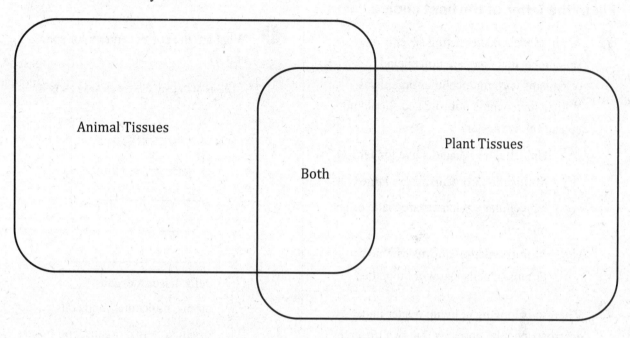

Animal Tissues

Both

Plant Tissues

❸ What are two benefits of multicellular organisms having some specialized cells rather than all the cells being the same?

_____

_____

_____

_____

❹ How can you compare a bicycle to an organism? Identify parts of a bicycle that are comparable to tissues, organs, and organ systems.

_____

_____

_____

_____

_____

Benchmark Assessment SC.6.L.14.1

Fill in the letter of the best choice.

1 Jemin made a poster listing several statements that compare unicellular organisms with multicellular organisms. Which statement is **not** true and should not appear on her poster?

Ⓐ Unicellular organisms live longer.

Ⓑ Multicellular organisms are larger.

Ⓒ Unicellular organisms are made of just one cell.

Ⓓ Multicellular organisms can have groups of cells that work together.

2 Theresa is looking at living matter under a microscope. She observes that two different types of cells are present in one structure. What is the **most** complex level of organization that Theresa is observing?

Ⓕ cell

Ⓖ molecule

Ⓗ organ

Ⓘ tissue

3 Xavier observes a group of similar cells that are working together to produce a substance. What kind of structure is he observing?

Ⓐ molecule

Ⓑ organ

Ⓒ organ system

Ⓓ tissue

4 What are the correct entries for spaces 2, 3, and 4?

Levels of Organization of an Animal's Body

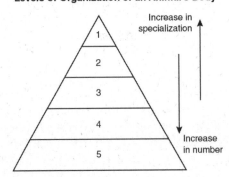

Ⓕ cells, tissues, organs

Ⓖ atoms, molecules, and cells

Ⓗ organ systems, organs, and tissues

Ⓘ organs, organ systems, and organisms

5 Green algae in the genus *Volvox* is formed by cells that join together. Each cell can survive on its own, but the cells work together to survive better. Which statement **correctly** explains how *Volvox* should be classified?

Ⓐ They are unicellular organisms because each cell can survive on its own.

Ⓑ They are unicellular organisms because each cell contains its own DNA.

Ⓒ They are unicellular organisms because each cell performs a different function.

Ⓓ They are unicellular organisms because each cell is part of a collection of cells.

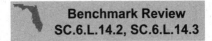

SC.6.L.14.2 Investigate and explain the components of the scientific theory of cells (cell theory): all organisms are composed of cells (single-celled or multi-cellular), all cells come from pre-existing cells, and cells are the basic unit of life. **SC.6.L.14.3** Recognize and explore how cells of all organisms undergo similar processes to maintain homeostasis, including extracting energy from food, getting rid of waste, and reproducing.

Characteristics of Cells

Cells Are Everywhere

Like all living things, you are made up of cells. A **cell** is the smallest functional and structural unit of all living organisms, and all organisms are made up of cells. Some organisms are just one cell. Others, such as humans, contain trillions of cells. An organism carries out all of its own life processes.

Organisms that are made up of just one cell are called *unicellular organisms*. The single cell of a unicellular organism must carry out all of the functions for life. Organisms that are made up of more than one cell are called *multicellular organisms*. The cells of multicellular organisms often have specialized structures and functions.

How Cells Were Discovered

In the early 1600s, nobody knew what a cell was. In 1665, a scientist named Robert Hooke built a microscope to look at tiny objects. One day, he looked at a thin slice of cork from the bark of a cork tree. The cork looked as if it was made of little boxes. Hooke named these boxes *cells*, which means "little rooms" in Latin. Around 1674, Anton van Leeuwenhoek became the first person to describe actual living cells when he looked at a drop of pond water under a microscope. He observed tiny organisms moving through the water. These early discoveries laid the foundations for what is known today as cell theory.

Plant Cells

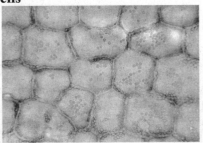

In 1838, Matthias Schleiden concluded that plants are made of cells. Then in 1839, Theodor Schwann determined that all animal tissues are made of cells. He concluded that all organisms are made up of one or more cells. Based on his observations about the cellular make up of organisms, Schwann made another conclusion. He determined that the cell is the basic unit of all living things. In 1858, Rudolf Virchow, a doctor, proposed that cells could form only from the division of other cells. The work of Schleiden, Schwann, and Virchow resulted in a scientific theory of cells.

The cell theory is fundamental to the study of organisms, medicine, heredity, evolution, and all other aspects of life science. Based on the evidence collected by scientists, the cell theory lists three basic characteristics of all cells and organisms:

- All organisms are made up of one or more cells.
- The cell is the basic unit of all organisms.
- All cells come from existing cells.

What Cells Have in Common

Scientific research has shown that cells are the basic unit of life. This means that cells carry out all of the functions necessary to keep an organism living. In order for cells to survive, they need to obtain and use energy, eliminate wastes, exchange materials, and make new cells. These processes allow cells to maintain the right balance of materials and conditions inside of themselves. The maintenance of a constant internal state in a changing environment is called **homeostasis**. Homeostasis allows cells and organisms to stay alive.

All living things need food to produce energy for cell processes. The process by which cells use oxygen to produce energy from food is called cellular respiration. Plants, animals, and most other organisms use cellular respiration to get energy from food.

Nearly all the oxygen around us is made by photosynthesis. Animals and plants use oxygen during cellular respiration to break down food. Cellular respiration also produces carbon dioxide. Plants need carbon dioxide to make sugars. So, photosynthesis and respiration are linked, each one depending on the products of the other.

Different cells vary in size and shape. However, all cells have some parts in common, including cell membranes, cytoplasm, organelles, and DNA. These different parts help the cell to carry out all the tasks needed for life.

How Cells Can Differ

Although cells have some basic parts in common, there are some important differences. The way that cells store their DNA is the main difference between the two cell types.

A **eukaryote** is an organism made up of cells that contain their DNA in a nucleus. All multicellular organisms are eukaryotes. Most eukaryotes are multicellular. Some eukaryotes, such as amoebas and yeasts, are unicellular. Eukaryotic cells contain membrane-bound organelles, as well as ribosomes.

eukaryotic cell

Not all eukaryotic cells are the same. Animals, plants, protists, and fungi are eukaryotes. Cells from these different types of organisms can be identified by some of their structures. For example, plants have a cell wall outside of their cell membrane, but

animal cells do not. Fungi cells have cell walls that are different from plant cell walls. Protist cells may or may not have cell walls. Plant cells are also distinguished by having chloroplasts, which allows them to perform photosynthesis.

prokaryotic cell

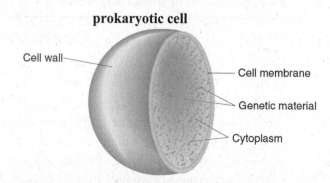

Cell wall — Cell membrane — Genetic material — Cytoplasm

A **prokaryote** is a single-celled organism that does not have a nucleus or membrane-bound organelles. Its DNA is located in the cytoplasm. Prokaryotic cells contain organelles called ribosomes that do not have a membrane. Some prokaryotic cells have hair-like structures called *flagella* that help them move. Prokaryotes, which include all bacteria and archaea, are almost always smaller than eukaryotes.

Cells Maintain Homeostasis

In order for cells to stay alive, they must maintain **homeostasis**, which is the maintenance of a constant internal state in a changing environment. They do this in similar ways. All cells require energy to perform their cell functions. Cells get energy from breaking down materials, such as food in which energy is stored. Plant cells make their own food through photosynthesis. They take in sunlight and change carbon dioxide and water into sugar and oxygen. Other organisms eat plants or other organisms that eat plants. Regardless of whether the organism makes its own food through photosynthesis or consumes another organism, they must all use oxygen to produce energy from their food. This is called **cellular respiration**.

It is also important that cells can get rid of wastes. This happens through the cell's membrane, which is semi-permeable. Only certain particles are allowed to cross the cell membrane. There are two types of transport through the cell membrane—

passive transport and active transport. **Passive transport** is the movement of particles across a cell membrane without the use of energy by the cell. One type of passive transport is called diffusion. This is when molecules move from high concentrations to low concentrations. Some waste products move out of the cell by diffusion. When cells need to move materials across the cell membrane from areas of low concentration to areas of higher concentration, they use active transport. **Active transport** is the movement of particles against a concentration gradient and requires the cell to use energy. Sometimes large particles require active transport to move them across a cell membrane.

Maintaining homeostasis also means that cells grow, divide and die. Multicellular organisms grow by adding more cells, which are made when existing cells divide. Some cells divide often to replace dead or damaged cells. Cell division is required for growth. Before the cell can divide, the DNA needs to be copied and separated. The DNA is packaged into chromosomes before they can divide. When equal numbers of chromosomes are separated, and the nucleus splits to form two identical nuclei, this is called **mitosis**. After mitosis occurs, the rest of the cell divides. Now there are two identical cells.

Student-Response Activity

1 Read each evidence statement. Which part of cell theory is supported by each piece of evidence?

Cells can be observed in plants, animals, fungi, protists, bacteria, and archaea.

_____

_____

A scientist observes two petri dishes. A colony of bacteria grows in one, and nothing grows in the other.

_____

_____

A single cell from a multicellular plant can be kept alive.

_____

_____

2 A scientist discovers a type of cell that produces a chemical, which is not useful to the cell. What can you conclude about the cell?

_____

_____

_____

_____

3 What are four things that cells can do to maintain homeostasis?

_____

_____

_____

_____

4 Use the terms listed in the word bank to fill in the blanks with the matching cell parts in each cell. Some terms may be used more than once.

Word Bank	**Eukaryotes**	**Prokaryotes**
cytoplasm	_____	_____
cell membrane	_____	_____
DNA in cytoplasm	_____	_____
DNA in nucleus	_____	_____
membrane-bound organelles	_____	_____
organelles		

5 Paul and Jessica are making a model of an animal cell. What should they show going into and out of the cell in their model?

_____

_____

_____

_____

_____

Benchmark Assessment SC.6.L.14.2, SC.6.L.14.3

Fill in the letter of the best choice.

1 Eukaryotic cells and prokaryotic cells have some parts in common. Which pairs of parts would you find in **both** types of cells?

- (A) cytoplasm and nucleus
- (B) cell membrane and cytoplasm
- (C) DNA and membrane-bound organelles
- (D) cell membrane and membrane-bound organelles

2 A virus is made of a protein shell that carries DNA. Which statement **best** describes how the virus can be classified according to cell theory?

- (F) It is an organism because it carries DNA.
- (G) It is an organism because it can replicate itself.
- (H) It is not an organism because it is not found in all living things.
- (I) It is not an organism because it does not carry out all the functions of life.

3 Anthony places a drop of water under a microscope and observes some small objects. He concludes that the small objects are cells. Which choice **most likely** describes the evidence that Anthony saw?

- (A) Anthony observed the objects moving in the water.
- (B) Anthony observed the objects changing size and shape.
- (C) Anthony observed the objects splitting into new objects.
- (D) Anthony observed the objects sticking to one another.

4 Scientists observe that colonies of cells appear after a single cell is placed on a petri dish. Which statement does this evidence **best** support?

- (F) Cells are able to reproduce.
- (G) Cells are the basic unit of life.
- (H) Cells are able to take in energy.
- (I) Cells are able to get rid of waste.

5 Cells in a multicellular organism are shown in the diagram.

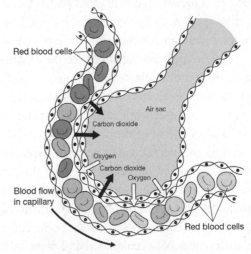

Red blood cells
Air sac
Carbon dioxide
Oxygen
Carbon dioxide
Oxygen
Blood flow in capillary
Red blood cells

Which statement **best** describes how all of the cells shown are similar?

- (A) They are all making new cells.
- (B) They are all transporting oxygen.
- (C) They are all doing photosynthesis.
- (D) They are all maintaining homeostasis.

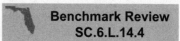

SC.6.L.14.4 Compare and contrast the structure and function of major organelles of plant and animal cells, including cell wall, cell membrane, nucleus, cytoplasm, chloroplasts, mitochondria, and vacuoles.

Cell Structure and Function

A Variety of Cells

All organisms are made up of one or more cells. Prokaryotes are made up of a single prokaryotic cell while eukaryotes are made up of one or more eukaryotic cells. Prokaryotic cells differ from eukaryotic cells in that they don't have a nucleus or membrane-bound organelles.

Eukaryotic cells can differ from each other depending on their structure and function. A cell's structure is the arrangement of its parts. A cell's function is the activity the parts carry out. For example, plant and animal cells have different parts that perform different functions for the organism. This is what makes plants and animals so different from each other. Even cells within the same organism can differ from each other depending on their function. Most of the cells in multicellular organisms are specialized to perform a specific function. However, all eukaryotic cells share some characteristics. These include a nucleus, membrane-bound organelles, and parts that protect and support the cell. The diagram below shows some similarities and differences between animal and plant cells.

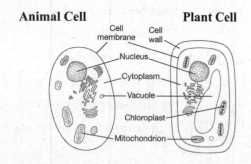

Cell Membrane

Every cell is surrounded by a cell membrane. The **cell membrane** acts as a barrier between the inside of a cell and the cell's environment. The cell membrane protects the cell and regulates what enters and leaves the cell.

Cell Wall

In addition to the cell membrane, plant cells have a cell wall. The **cell wall** is a rigid structure that surrounds the cell membrane. Cell walls provide support and protection to the cell. Plants don't have a skeleton like many animals do, so they get their shape from the cell wall. The cells of fungi, archaea, bacteria, and some protists also have cell walls.

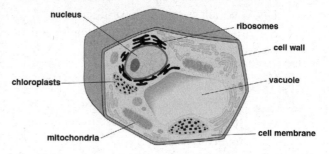

Nucleus

The nucleus is an organelle in eukaryotic cells that contains the cell's genetic material. Deoxyribonucleic acid, or DNA, is stored in the nucleus. DNA is genetic material that contains information needed for cell processes, such as making proteins. Proteins perform most actions of a cell. Although DNA is found in the nucleus, proteins are not made there. Instead, instructions for how to make proteins are stored in DNA. These instructions are sent out of the nucleus through pores in the nuclear membrane. The nuclear membrane is a double layer. Each layer is similar in structure to the cell membrane.

Cytoplasm

The **cytoplasm** is the region between the cell membrane and the nucleus that includes fluid and all of the organelles. Throughout the cytoplasm of eukaryotic cells is a cytoskeleton. The cytoskeleton is a network of protein filaments that gives shape and support to cells. The cytoskeleton is also involved in cell division and in movement. It may help parts within the cell to move. Or it may form structures that help the whole organism to move.

Chloroplasts

Animals must eat food to provide their cells with energy. However, plants, and some protists, can make their own food using photosynthesis. These organisms have **chloroplasts**, organelles where photosynthesis occurs. Photosynthesis is the process by which cells use sunlight, carbon dioxide, and water to make sugar and oxygen. Chloroplasts are green because they contain a green pigment called chlorophyll. Chlorophyll absorbs the energy in sunlight. This energy is used to make sugar, which is then used by mitochondria to make a molecule called adenosine triphosphate, or ATP. Similar to mitochondria, chloroplasts have two membranes and their own DNA.

Mitochondria

Organisms need energy for life processes. Cells carry out such processes for growth and repair, movement of materials into and out of the cell, and chemical processes. Cells get energy by breaking down food using a process called cellular respiration. Cellular respiration occurs in an organelle called the mitochondrion. In cellular respiration, cells use oxygen to release energy stored in food. For example, cells break down the sugar glucose to release the energy stored in the sugar. The mitochondria then transfer the energy released from the sugar to ATP. Cells use ATP to carry out cell processes.

Mitochondria have their own DNA and they have two membranes. The outer membrane is smooth. The inner membrane has many folds. Folds increase the surface area inside the mitochondria where cellular respiration occurs.

Vacuoles

A **vacuole** is a fluid-filled vesicle found in the cells of most animals, plants, and fungi. A vacuole may contain enzymes, nutrients, water, or wastes. Plant cells also have a large central vacuole that stores water. Central vacuoles full of water help support the cell. Plants may wilt when the central vacuole loses water.

Animal cells also have other structures similar to vacuoles called lysosomes. Lysosomes contain digestive enzymes, which break down worn-out or damaged organelles, waste materials, and foreign invaders in the cell. Some of these materials are collected in vacuoles. A lysosome attaches to the vacuole and releases the digestive enzymes inside. Some of these materials are recycled and reused in the cell. For example, a human liver cell recycles half of its materials each week.

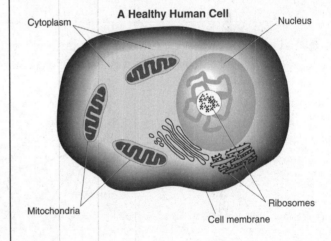

A Healthy Human Cell

Cytoplasm · Nucleus · Mitochondria · Ribosomes · Cell membrane

Student-Response Activity

1 Identify whether these statements describe an *animal cell*, a *plant cell*, or *both*.

nucleus: contains genetic material _____

lysosomes: helps to break down particles _____

chloroplasts: performs photosynthesis _____

mitochondria: releases energy through cellular respiration _____

cell wall: provides shape and support _____

cell membrane: separates the cell from its surroundings _____

central vacuole: stores water and helps support the cell _____

2 What are two adaptations in plant cells that do similar things for plants as bones do for animals?

_____

_____

3 The cell shown in the diagram is a protist called euglena. Early scientists were not sure how to classify this organism. What is one way that euglena cells are similar to plant cells, and one way they are similar to animal cells?

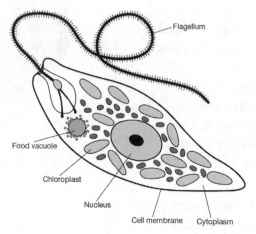

_____

4 How are lysosomes similar to vacuoles?

_____

_____

5 A deer eats a leaf from a tree and gets energy from sugar molecules in the leaf. Which two organelles are required to make this process possible?

_____

Benchmark Assessment SC.6.L.14.4

Fill in the letter of the best choice.

❶ Rasheeda made a model of a plant cell and labeled parts of the cell that are **not** found in animal cells. Which other part of the cell should Rasheeda label?

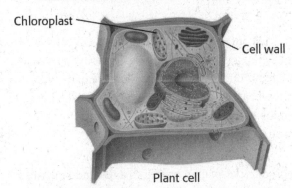

Chloroplast

Cell wall

Plant cell

(A) cytoplasm

(B) large central vacuole

(C) lysosomes

(D) mitochondria

❷ Which choice **best** describes an animal cell?

(F) a cell that does not use sugars

(G) a cell that does not have a nucleus

(H) a cell that does not have a cell wall

(I) a cell that does not have a cell membrane

❸ Which statement **best** describes the function of the nucleus?

(A) to hold a plant cell's DNA

(B) to hold an animal cell's DNA

(C) to hold all types of cells' DNA

(D) to hold both plant and animal cells' DNA

❹ Which is **true** of only animal cells?

(F) Their cytoplasm contains organelles.

(G) They do not have a rigid outermost layer.

(H) The process of obtaining energy requires sugar.

(I) They have organelles that are surrounded by membranes.

❺ Ernest was looking at the following diagram of a cell. Which statement **best** explains how he should classify the cell?

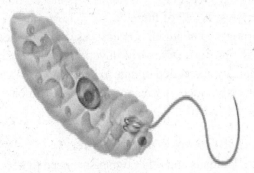

(A) He should classify the cell as a plant cell because it has a cell membrane.

(B) He should classify the cell as an animal cell because it has a flagellum.

(C) He should classify the cell as a plant cell because it has cytoplasm.

(D) He should not classify the cell as either a plant cell or an animal cell.

SC.6.L.14.5 Identify and investigate the general functions of the major systems of the human body (digestive, respiratory, circulatory, reproductive, excretory, immune, nervous, and musculoskeletal) and describe ways these systems interact with each other to maintain homeostasis.
SC.6.L.14.6 Compare and contrast types of infectious agents that may infect the human body, including viruses, bacteria, fungi, and parasites.

Human Body Systems

Systems in the Body

Our bodies are like incredibly complex machines. They can do some amazing things, but many parts must work together to make sure that they function properly. The human body is a system, meaning that it is made of a collection of parts that work together. In fact, the human body is a system made up of a collection of smaller systems, called organ systems. The human body requires that all of these organ systems work correctly to maintain homeostasis. Similarly, each of the organ systems within your body depends on smaller parts called organs to keep them working correctly. Some organs work in more than one organ system.

Body Systems Work Together

Humans and other organisms need to get energy. They need to use energy to run their bodies and move. They need to reproduce. They need to get rid of waste and protect their bodies. Organ systems help organisms to do all of these things. They also coordinate all the functions of a body. Organ systems in the human body include:

Digestive System: Your digestive system breaks down the food you eat into nutrients that can be used by the body. Chewing, a type of mechanical digestion, breaks down food into smaller pieces that are easier to swallow and digest. The stomach grinds food into a pulpy mixture. Nutrients are absorbed in the small intestine where most chemical digestion takes place.

Respiratory System: This system is responsible for gathering oxygen from the environment and gets ride of carbon dioxide from the body. This exchange happens in the lungs.

Circulatory System: This system carries nutrients, gases, and hormones to body cells and waste products from body cells. It is made up of the heart, blood vessels, and blood. The heart pumps blood through the body. Blood flows through blood vessels.

Reproductive System: The female reproductive system produces eggs and nourishes and protects the fetus. The male reproductive system produces and delivers sperm.

Excretory System: Your kidneys remove wastes from the blood and regulate your body's fluids. The skin, lungs, and digestive system also remove wastes from the body.

Immune System: The immune system returns leaked fluids to blood vessels and helps get rid of bacteria and viruses.

Nervous System: Your brain, spinal cord, and nerves collect information and respond to it by sending electrical messages throughout your body. This information may come from outside or inside the body. The brain is the center of the nervous system. Your body senses the environment with specialized structures called sensory organs, which include the eyes, the skin, the ears, the mouth, and the nose.

Musculoskeletal System: Your muscular system works with the skeletal system to help you move. Your skeletal system, which is made up of bones, ligaments, and cartilage, supports the body and protects important organs. It also makes blood cells.

Endocrine System: Your glands send out chemical messages. Ovaries and testes are part of this system.

The Endocrine System

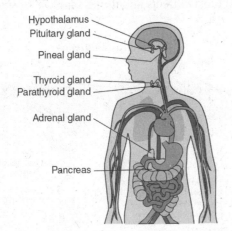

Hypothalamus
Pituitary gland
Pineal gland
Thyroid gland
Parathyroid gland
Adrenal gland
Pancreas

Our body systems can do a lot, but they cannot work alone! Almost everything we need for our bodies to work properly requires many body systems to work together. For example, the nervous system may sense danger. Nerves detect a stimulus in the environment and send a signal through the spinal cord to the brain. The brain sends a signal to respond. The endocrine system releases hormones that cause the heart to beat faster to deliver more oxygen through the circulatory system to muscles. The musculoskeletal system works to run away from danger.

Body Systems Communicate

In order to work together, body systems have to communicate. There are two basic ways they can communicate: by electrical messages and by chemical messages. Nerve cells transfer information between the body and the spinal cord and brain. Nerves pass electrical messages from one cell to the next along the line. The endocrine system sends chemical messages through the bloodstream to certain cells. Because chemicals are distinct from each other, cells, organs, and organ systems can respond to chemicals differently.

Homeostasis

Like cells, your body must maintain **homeostasis**, or the maintenance of a constant internal environment when outside conditions change. Your body needs to have the right

amounts of water, oxygen, nutrients, and warmth in order to function properly. Your body systems constantly work together to make sure these needs are being met.

If any body system fails to function properly, homeostasis may be disrupted. For example, a problem in the digestive system can cause the body to have a lack of nutrients. A lack of food harms many systems and may cause disease or even death. The presence of toxins or pathogens also can disrupt homeostasis. Toxins can prevent cells from carrying out life processes and pathogens can break down cells. Problems also occur if the body's messages do not work, or they are not sent when or where they are needed. Many diseases which affect homeostasis are hereditary.

Infection

Homeostasis in your body can be disrupted by harmful things in the environment. Microscopic organisms and particles, such as bacteria and viruses, are all around you. Most are harmless, but some can make you sick. Thankfully, our bodies have ways of protecting us against harmful agents such as these. Your skin provides external protection against pathogens that may enter the body. Most of the time, pathogens cannot get past external defenses. Sometimes, skin is cut and pathogens can enter the body. Your body may respond by raising your body temperature. This response is called fever, which slows the growth of bacteria and some other pathogens. If a pathogen is not destroyed by fever, then the immune system responds.

Noninfectious and Infectious Diseases

When you have a disease, your body does not function normally. Diseases cause specific symptoms, or changes in how a person feels. The many types of diseases can be categorized as either noninfectious or infectious.

Diseases that are caused by hereditary or environmental factors are called **noninfectious diseases**. For example, cystic fibrosis is caused by hereditary factors. People with cystic fibrosis inherited a mutated gene from each of their parents. The gene causes excess mucus to build up in the lungs, pancreas, and other organs. This excess mucus can lead to infections and damage to organs. Other types of noninfectious diseases can be caused by environmental factors. Mutagens are environmental factors that cause mutations, or changes, in DNA. Sometimes, the changes cause a cell to reproduce uncontrollably. This results in a disease called cancer.

A disease that is caused by a pathogen is called an **infectious disease**. Pathogens include bacteria, fungi, and parasites, which are all alive. Pathogens also include viruses, which are noncellular particles that depend on living things to reproduce. Viruses are not considered to be alive because they cannot function on their own. A disease that spreads from person to person is a contagious disease. Diseases can be transmitted to people by other people, by other organisms and by contaminated food, water, or objects.

Types of Pathogens

Viruses are tiny particles that have their own genetic material but depend on living things to reproduce. Viruses insert their genetic material into a cell, and then the cell makes more viruses. The diagram shows how viruses destroy cells in the process of replicating themselves.

Bacteria are single-celled prokaryotic organisms. Most bacteria are beneficial to other living things. However, some bacteria cause

disease. For example, the bacterium that causes tuberculosis infects about one-third of the world's population.

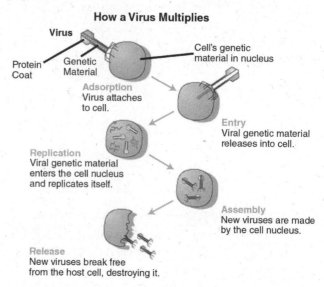

How a Virus Multiplies

Adsorption Virus attaches to cell.

Entry Viral genetic material releases into cell.

Replication Viral genetic material enters the cell nucleus and replicates itself.

Assembly New viruses are made by the cell nucleus.

Release New viruses break free from the host cell, destroying it.

Some fungi are pathogens, but most fungi are beneficial. Fungi decompose, or break down, dead plants and animals into materials that other organisms use. A fungus that infects a living organism will damage the organism. The most common fungal diseases are skin infections.

A parasite is an organism that lives on and feeds on another organism, called a host. Parasites usually harm the host. Some of the most common parasites in humans are certain types of single-celled organisms called protists. For example, the protists that cause malaria infect as many as 500 million people each year.

Student-Response Activity

❶ What are four types of pathogens that can cause infectious disease?

_____

_____

_____

② How are fungi and bacteria both similar to and different from one another? Answer by completing the Venn diagram.

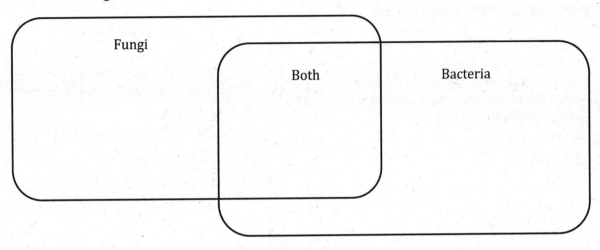

Fungi

Both

Bacteria

❸ All cells need oxygen to function properly. Which body systems need to coordinate to make sure cells receive oxygen?

_____

_____

❹ Jackie sees a tree branch about to fall on her, and she jumps out of the way. Which body systems helped her respond to danger?

_____

_____

❺ What is one example of an organ that is part of multiple body systems? Tell which body systems the organ is part of.

_____

_____

_____

❻ The stomach is part of the digestive system. Which other body systems would be affected if the stomach no longer functioned properly?

_____

_____

_____

Benchmark Assessment SC.6.L.14.5, SC.6.L.14.6

Fill in the letter of the best choice.

1 Marnee goes to the doctor because she has been coughing and sneezing. The doctor explains that a pathogen entered her cells and started replicating, which caused her to get sick. What was the cause of Marnee's sickness?

(A) bacteria

(B) fungi

(C) protists

(D) virus

2 The liver regulates how much sugar enters the bloodstream. What body systems is the liver a part of?

(F) digestive and excretory systems

(G) circulatory and digestive systems

(H) respiratory and endocrine systems

(I) musculoskeletal and integumentary systems

3 Kendrick made a model that included kidneys, liver, large intestine, and bladder. What is the **main** function of the body system that Kendrick built a model of?

(A) It gets rid of wastes that the body produces.

(B) It uses electrical signals to control body functions.

(C) It uses chemical messages to control body functions.

(D) It gets rid of pathogens that invade the body.

4 James made a poster showing the two body systems that regulate a person's pulse. Which two systems did James represent on his poster?

(F) nervous and circulatory systems

(G) respiratory and endocrine systems

(H) circular and digestive systems

(I) digestive and nervous systems

5 The endocrine system consists of many glands that produce chemical messages. These chemicals are sent to organs throughout the body. Which system works with the endocrine system to deliver the chemical messages to the body?

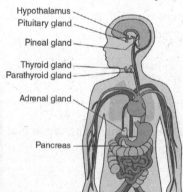

The Endocrine System

Hypothalamus
Pituitary gland
Pineal gland
Thyroid gland
Parathyroid gland
Adrenal gland
Pancreas

(A) circulatory system

(B) excretory system

(C) nervous system

(D) respiratory system

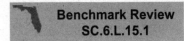
SC.6.L.15.1 Analyze and describe how and why organisms are classified according to shared characteristics with emphasis on the Linnaean system combined with the concept of Domains.

Classification of Living Things

The Tree of Life

There are millions of kinds of living things on Earth. How do scientists keep all of these living things organized? Scientists classify living things based on characteristics that living things share. Classification helps scientists answer questions such as:

- How many kinds of living things are there?
- What characteristics define each kind of living thing?
- What are the relationships among living things?

Scientists investigate these questions systematically. Using evidence gathered from many observations, scientists have developed hypotheses about how different living things are related. These hypotheses are often represented by a "tree of life" diagram. These diagrams, also called cladograms, show the relationships among organisms by a series of branching lines.

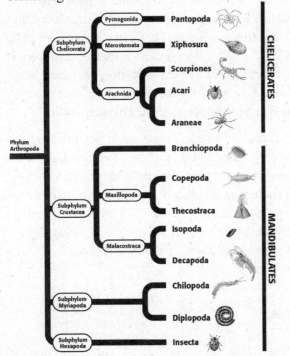

Scientists frequently debate how cladograms should be arranged, and new evidence frequently leads scientists to revise them. There is no one correct way to draw a tree of life, but they are still very useful. The cladogram here shows a hypothesis about how some arthropods are related.

Shared Characteristics

There are many animals on Earth that look similar. If two organisms look similar, are they related? Scientists have to look at many characteristics to decide whether or not two organisms are related. Scientists must compare physical characteristics, such as size or bone structure. Scientists also compare the chemical characteristics of living things.

Physical Characteristics

Scientists look at physical characteristics, such as skeletal structure. They also study how organisms develop from an egg to an adult. Organisms that have similar skeletons and development may be related. Kangaroos and mice, for instance, both have legs, hair, and a dorsal nerve cord, but the nature of development is different and their bipedal posture is different.

Chemical Characteristics

Scientists can identify the relationships among organisms by studying genetic material such as DNA and RNA. They use mutations and genetic similarities to find relationships among organisms. Organisms that have very similar gene sequences or have the same mutations are likely related. Other chemicals, such as proteins and hormones, can also be studied to learn how organisms are related.

Putting It All Together

The first scientist to systematically organize living things by their traits was a Swedish botanist named Carl Linnaeus. Linnaeus's ideas became the basis for modern taxonomy. **Taxonomy** is the science of describing, classifying, and naming living things. The way that scientists classify organisms today is based on the Linnaean system. The Linnaean system of classification is a hierarchy, or a system in which groups are put together and ranked. Linnaeus's original system had seven ranks. Linnaeus lived and worked in the 1700s. Since then, about 2 million new species have been described, and our understanding of the history of life has expanded greatly. As a result, the Linnaean system has had to expand as well. Today, scientists recognize many more levels above, between, and even below the original seven.

Below the level of kingdom, organisms are grouped into a phylum, class, order, family, genus, and species, as well as levels in between each of these.

Domains and Kingdoms

For Linnaeus, the kingdom was the highest level of organization. The highest rank in the modern system of classification is the domain. Carl Woese introduced domains. He realized that the previous kingdom system did not show similarities and differences between the eukaryotes and bacteria. A **domain** includes the greatest number of different organisms within it. All living things are grouped into one of three domains: Bacteria, Archae, and Eukarya. Human beings are in the domain Eukarya, along with fish, ferns, yeast, and amoebas, to name a few. The domain Bacteria is made up of prokaryotes that usually have a cell wall and reproduce by cell division. The domain Archae is also made up of prokaryotes, but they differ from bacteria in their genetics and the makeup of their cell walls. The domain Eukarya has cells with a nucleus and membrane-bound organelles.

The next rank below domain is kingdom. Eukarya has four kingdoms: Animalia, Plantae, Fungi, and Protista. Humans and fish are in the kingdom Animalia together. Ferns, yeasts, and amoebas are all in different kingdoms. That means that humans are more like fish than they are like amoebas, fungi, or plants.

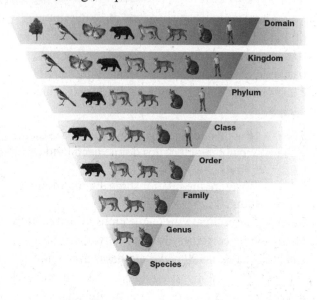

Genus and Species

Any organism that you can think of is a particular species. A species is the basic unit of classification. A **species** is a group of organisms that are very closely related. They can mate and produce fertile offspring. There are more species than there are any other levels of classification. Members of a species share all of the same characteristics, though there can be variation in those characteristics.

Lions, for example, may look very different from each other, but they all share certain traits that make them different from any other organism. Lions also share many traits with tigers, but the two species have many differences as well. Lions and tigers are members of closely related species. This makes them members of a common genus, *Panthera*.

A scientific name always includes the genus name followed by the specific name. The first letter of the genus name is capitalized, and the first letter of the specific name is lowercased. The entire scientific name is written either in italics or underlined. Consider the scientific name for a lion: *Panthera leo.* The first part, *Panthera*, is the genus name. A genus includes similar species. The second part, *leo*, is the specific, or species name. No other species is named *Panthera leo.*

Student-Response Activity

1 What are the eight main levels of classification from most general to most definite?

_____

_____

_____

_____

_____

_____

_____

2 Dr. Nick is describing a new species he discovered. He says it is large enough to see without a lens and it eats small plants. What domain and kingdom is the organism **most likely** in?

_____

_____

Name ________________________________ Date ____________

3 Margaret tells her friends that she caught a fish called *Salmo salar*. What genus does the fish belong to? Explain how you know.

____

____

____

____

4 A scientist finds a tiny fragment of a bone too small to be classified by its appearance. The scientist studies the tiny fragment and concludes that it belonged to an ancient primate species. How was the scientist able to classify the bone?

____

____

____

____

5 Look at the diagram. Do both lemurs and humans have the traits listed at point D? Explain your reasoning.

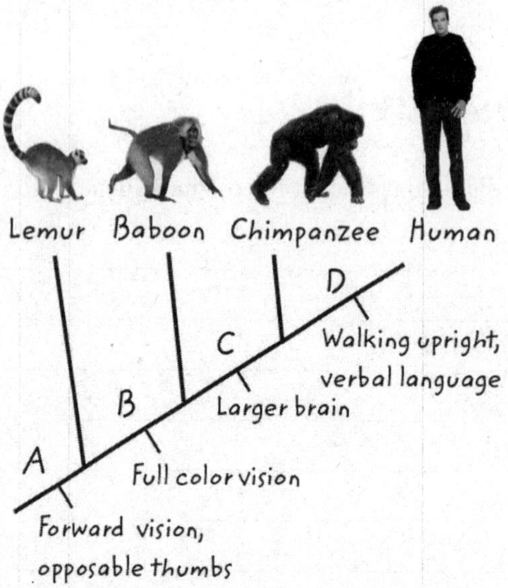
Lemur
Baboon
Chimpanzee
Human
A
B
C
D
Forward vision,
opposable thumbs
Full color vision
Larger brain
Walking upright,
verbal language

____

____

____

____

____

____

Benchmark Assessment SC.6.L.15.1

Fill in the letter of the best choice.

1 A scientist finds an organism that cannot move. It has many cells, produces spores, and gets food from its environment. In which kingdom does it belong?

(A) kingdom Animalia

(B) kingdom Fungi

(C) kingdom Plantae

(D) kingdom Protista

2 A student is building a model showing how living things are organized. Which pair of groups contains the greatest number of organisms?

(F) genus and species

(G) phylum and class

(H) domain and genus

(I) domain and kingdom

3 Two different kinds of organisms are as closely related as possible. Which statement is **most likely** true about the organisms?

(A) They are in the same genus.

(B) They are in the same species.

(C) They share the same DNA.

(D) They share no common ancestors.

4 Jessica learns that two organisms are members of the same class. Which can she also infer is **true**?

(F) The organisms are members of the same order.

(G) The organisms are members of the same family.

(H) The organisms are members of the same genus.

(I) The organisms are members of the same phylum.

5 Serena knows that scientists use physical characteristics to classify organisms. She studies the figures of four different organisms.

1   2   3   4

Which two organisms should Serena conclude are **most** closely related?

(A) 1 and 2

(B) 1 and 3

(C) 2 and 3

(D) 2 and 4

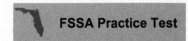
FSSA Practice Test–Form A

Instructions–Form A

The following pages contain a practice test. Do not look at the test until your teacher tells you to begin.

Use the answer sheet on page 87 to mark your answers.

Read each question carefully. Restate the question in your own words.

Watch for key words such as **best, not, most, least** and **except**.

A question might include one or more tables, graphs, diagrams, or pictures. Study these carefully before choosing an answer.

For Questions 1–40, find the best answer. Fill in the answer bubble for that answer. Do not make any stray marks around answer spaces.

1 Mammals are complex organisms whose bodies are highly organized. Which choice lists levels of organization in mammals from least organized to most organized?

A cells → molecules → atoms

B cells → tissues → organs

C molecules → tissues → cells

D organs → tissues → cells

2 Mike and Jamie are making a model to show how the human body is organized.

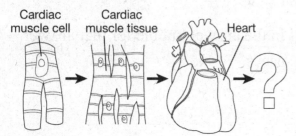

Cardiac muscle cell   Cardiac muscle tissue   Heart

Which level of organization comes next?

F organ

G organelle

H organism

I organ system

3 A doctor is examining an unknown sample and concludes that it is a tissue. Which **most likely** explains why the doctor made that conclusion?

A The sample contained cytoplasm and organelles.

B The sample had a membrane and a nucleus.

C The sample was made of a group of similar cells.

D The sample was made of two kinds of cells.

4 The scientific theory of cells is important to all branches of biology. Which statement **best** explains why?

F All of life's processes happen inside of cells.

G Many organisms are composed of cells.

H All living things must consume cells to survive.

I Cells are the basic units of all living things.

5 Cells must maintain homeostasis in order to survive. Which choice is **not** an example of how cells maintain homeostasis?

A Cells eliminate waste.

B Cells make specialized structures.

C Cells regulate chemicals.

D Cells take in food.

6 The diagram shows structures found in a plant cell.

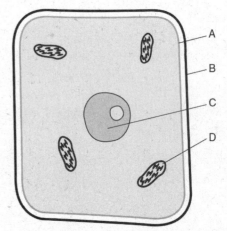

Which structure is shared by **all** types of cells?

F A

G B

H C

I D

7 Angie looked under a microscope and saw cells that contain a relatively large structure filled with water. She concluded she was observing a plant cell. Why did she draw that conclusion?

A She observed a central vacuole.

B She observed a chloroplast.

C She observed a lysosome.

D She observed a nucleus.

8 Tracy was making a list of structures in an animal cell. Which should she **not** include in her list?

F chloroplast

G cytoplasm

H mitochondria

I nucleus

9 Every cell in the human body needs oxygen to survive. Which two body systems are **mostly** responsible for getting oxygen to human cells?

A digestive and excretory

B muscular and nervous

C reproductive and respiratory

D respiratory and circulatory

10 If a person eats food containing tapeworm eggs or larvae, the tapeworm can enter the intestines and grow there. This image shows a tapeworm.

Which type of organism is a tapeworm?

F bacterium

G fungus

H parasite

I virus

11 Organisms are grouped with similar organisms. Within groups, there may be other less inclusive groups, which contain fewer types of organisms. Which is the **least** inclusive group that contains both humans and plants?

A domain

B kingdom

C order

D phylum

12 Vidya made a presentation to her class about the organism *Lemur catta*. Which statement is **true**?

F It is in the genus *catta*.

G It is in the genus *Lemur*.

H It is in the kingdom Eukarya.

I It is in the kingdom Mammalia.

13 Florida's rivers contribute to the processes of weathering, erosion, and deposition. Which Florida land feature is **most likely** the result of deposition by rivers?

A coastlines

B deltas

C dunes

D lakes

14 The processes of weathering, erosion, and deposition are continuously reshaping Earth's surface. Which is an example of erosion?

F A sea cave is formed by ocean waves degrading softer rocks.

G Loose dirt on a mountainside is moved downhill by wind and gravity.

H Upward pressure caused by a shift in Earth's crust forms a mountain.

I Over time, a sandbar forms in the ocean from particles carried by a river.

15 While on a trip, Joshua saw the landform shown this image.

Which processes formed this landform?

A the transport and deposition of sediment by gravity

B the transport and deposition of sediment by ice

C the transport and deposition of sediment by water

D the transport and deposition of sediment by wind

16 What type of energy transfer is occurring when cooler air molecules come into direct contact with the warm ground and energy is passed to the air?

F conduction

G convection

H radiation

I uplift

17 Which process brings heat and light from the sun to Earth?

A conduction

B convection

C magnetism

D radiation

18 Oceans have an effect on weather in the form of hurricanes. Warm ocean water fuels hurricanes.

Which conditions contribute to the decrease in a hurricane's strength as it moves from the ocean onto land?

F abundance of moist air over land

G rising hot air from the land

H sinking hot air from the land

I the lack of warm, moist air over land

19 Which **best** describes how the sun causes wind?

A The sun heats the Earth unevenly, causing warm air to rise and cool air to sink, which causes differences in air pressure.

B The sun heats the Earth evenly, which causes all air to rise.

C The sun heats the Earth unevenly, causing warm air to sink and cool air to rise, which causes differences in air pressure.

D The sun heats the Earth evenly, which causes all air to sink.

20 Juliana measures the outdoor temperature each day for a week at exactly 3:00 P.M. The temperatures she records are all between 25 °C and 30 °C. Juliana concludes that the climate of her area is tropical. What is the **most** important reason why her conclusion may **not** be correct?

F She did not calculate the humidity, air pressure, and wind conditions.

G She made her conclusion based only on temperature and did not include precipitation.

H She made her conclusion based on only one week of data instead of over a long period of time.

I She recorded the temperature at only one time of day instead of more often.

21 Carly draws a map of surface currents in the Atlantic Ocean. On her map, she includes the major wind belts for the same area. Her map is similar to the one shown below.

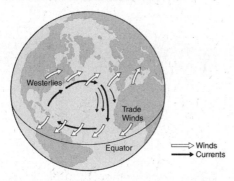

If Carly wants to add wind belts for the part of the Atlantic just south of the equator, how should she draw the arrows?

A The arrows should curve downward to the left.

B The arrows should curve downward to the right.

C The arrows should curve upward to the left.

D The arrows should curve upward to the right.

22 Which is the **best** indicator of an area's climate?

F The recorded temperature and precipitation for 100 years.

G The recorded temperature and precipitation for 1 month.

H The recorded temperature for 100 years.

I The recorded precipitation for 1 month.

23 Which question is **least likely** to be useful when investigating a scientific theory?

A Has the data presented been tested with further observations?

B Have television and radio stations investigated the theory?

C Is there any evidence that contradicts the explanation or claim?

D What were the methods used to collect the data?

24 Which **best** describes how a scientific theory is different from a guess or hunch?

F A scientific theory is well supported and widely accepted.

G A guess or hunch is well supported and widely accepted.

H A scientific theory is a claim posed by an individual.

I A guess or hunch is agreed upon by most scientists.

25 Ginny enjoys mountain climbing. Today, she is climbing Mt. Sheridan, which is the tallest mountain she has ever climbed. When Ginny makes it to the top, she notices that it is more difficult to catch her breath. At higher elevations, why is it harder for Ginny to breathe?

A At higher altitudes, the air contains too much carbon dioxide.

B At higher altitudes, the air contains too much nitrogen.

C At higher altitudes, the air is too cold.

D At higher altitudes, the air pressure is lower.

26 The following diagram shows a ball at different points on a ramp.

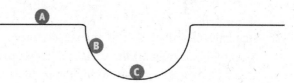

At which point does the ball have almost equal amounts of kinetic and potential energy?

F A

G B

H C

I A and C

27 This roller coaster shows a roller coaster car at various points along the ride.

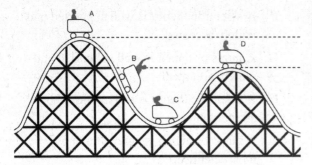

Why might the first hill on many roller coaster rides be the highest?

A The high potential energy at the start can help the roller coaster climb the next hills if they are lower than the first one.

B The roller coaster will convert kinetic energy into potential energy after the first hill, so the car must have the least potential energy at the start.

C The roller coaster will have more potential energy as it progresses through the ride, so the car must have the least potential energy at the start.

D The total energy of the roller coaster will increase as the ride progresses, so the car must have the most potential energy at the start.

28 One ball rolls along a shelf at a steady rate. A second ball rolls off the shelf and gains speed as it falls in a curved path. Which must have an unbalanced force acting on it?

F both balls

G neither balls

H the ball that falls

I the ball that rolls along the shelf

29 A distance-time graph plots the distance traveled by an object and the time it takes to travel that distance.

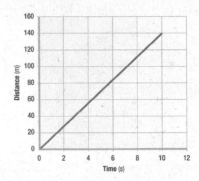

Which **best** describes how this object is moving?

A accelerating

B at a constant speed

C slowing down

D stopped

30 Zoe planned to conduct an investigation to find out what can cause an object to change its speed, direction, or both. What should she include in her investigation?

F an object at rest

G an object on which balanced forces are acting

H an object on which unbalanced forces are acting

I an object with a large mass

31 Two identical space probes are orbiting Jupiter. Scientists determine that one of the space probes has a larger gravitational force acting on it than the other. Which is the **most likely** reason for the difference?

A One space probe has more air resistance than the other.

B One space probe is closer to Jupiter than the other.

C One space probe reached Jupiter before the other.

D Only one space probe is exerting a gravitational force on the other.

32 Which is **not** a characteristic of good scientific investigations?

   F   They are open to questions.

   G   They are replicable.

   H   They are used to develop a theory.

   I   They follow accepted methods of investigation.

33 Luis is trying to push a box of new soccer balls across the floor. In the illustration, the arrow on the box represents the force that Luis exerts.

If the box is not moving, which must be **true**?

   A   Luis is applying a force that acts at a distance.

   B   The box is exerting a larger force on Luis than he is exerting on the box.

   C   There is another force acting on the box that balances Luis's force.

   D   There is no force of friction acting on the box.

34 Gravity is a force of attraction between objects that is due to their masses. Which statement is **true** about gravity?

   F   It affects only large objects in space.

   G   It affects only objects that touch.

   H   It exists between all objects in the universe.

   I   It exists only between Earth and the sun.

35 Raul wants to investigate how the angle of a ramp affects the speed of an object rolling down the ramp. He can conduct his investigation in a number of different ways. Which investigation should he perform?

   A   observe different bicyclists riding down hills of varying steepness

   B   observe video of various objects rolling down hills and estimate the angle of the hill and the speed of the object

   C   perform an experiment in a lab in which the angle of the ramp is controlled and the speed of a rolling cart is measured

   D   record the time it takes one bicyclist to ride down hills of varying steepness

36 Scientists do many types of work. Their work often includes making field observations, conducting surveys, creating models, and carrying out experiments. Which characterizes an experiment?

   F   an organized procedure to study something under controlled conditions

   G   collection of data from the unregulated world for comparative purposes

   H   observation of plants or animals in their natural environment

   I   physical or mathematical representation of an object or process

37 Lee wants to make sure he understands the components of a good scientific investigation. He knows that it should be controlled and have a large sample size. Also, he thinks that the results should be communicated to other scientists. Which is another component that is necessary for a good investigation?

   A   It must be able to be replicated by other scientists.

   B   It must be conducted in a big lab.

   C   It must be done with expensive equipment.

   D   It must be run by a university scientist.

38 Three different lab groups perform experiments to determine the density of the samples of iron. They have all rounded the density to the nearest whole number.

Group	Mass of iron (g)	Volume of iron (cm³)	Density of iron (g/cm³)
1	32	4	8
2	48	6	8
3	?	5	8

What is the mass of iron for group 3?

F 5 g

G 8 g

H 40 g

I 64 g

39 What might cause a theory or model to change?

A articles on the Internet

B multiple scientists disagree

C new evidence

D one experiment at a university laboratory

40 The diagram shows Neils Bohr's theory about how electrons are arranged in atoms. He thought electrons traveled on specific paths around a nucleus. The current theory is that electrons exist in certain cloudlike regions around a nucleus.

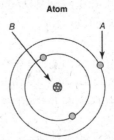

Atom

How would a model of the current theory differ from Bohr's model?

F Both objects A and B would differ from Bohr's model.

G It would be the same as Bohr's model.

H Object A would differ from Bohr's model.

I Object B would differ from Bohr's model.

Florida Statewide Science Assessment Preparation Practice Test—Form A

Mark one answer for each question.

1 Ⓐ Ⓑ Ⓒ Ⓓ   21 Ⓐ Ⓑ Ⓒ Ⓓ
2 Ⓕ Ⓖ Ⓗ Ⓘ   22 Ⓕ Ⓖ Ⓗ Ⓘ
3 Ⓐ Ⓑ Ⓒ Ⓓ   23 Ⓐ Ⓑ Ⓒ Ⓓ
4 Ⓕ Ⓖ Ⓗ Ⓘ   24 Ⓕ Ⓖ Ⓗ Ⓘ
5 Ⓐ Ⓑ Ⓒ Ⓓ   25 Ⓐ Ⓑ Ⓒ Ⓓ
6 Ⓕ Ⓖ Ⓗ Ⓘ   26 Ⓕ Ⓖ Ⓗ Ⓘ
7 Ⓐ Ⓑ Ⓒ Ⓓ   27 Ⓐ Ⓑ Ⓒ Ⓓ
8 Ⓕ Ⓖ Ⓗ Ⓘ   28 Ⓕ Ⓖ Ⓗ Ⓘ
9 Ⓐ Ⓑ Ⓒ Ⓓ   29 Ⓐ Ⓑ Ⓒ Ⓓ
10 Ⓕ Ⓖ Ⓗ Ⓘ   30 Ⓕ Ⓖ Ⓗ Ⓘ
11 Ⓐ Ⓑ Ⓒ Ⓓ   31 Ⓐ Ⓑ Ⓒ Ⓓ
12 Ⓕ Ⓖ Ⓗ Ⓘ   32 Ⓕ Ⓖ Ⓗ Ⓘ
13 Ⓐ Ⓑ Ⓒ Ⓓ   33 Ⓐ Ⓑ Ⓒ Ⓓ
14 Ⓕ Ⓖ Ⓗ Ⓘ   34 Ⓕ Ⓖ Ⓗ Ⓘ
15 Ⓐ Ⓑ Ⓒ Ⓓ   35 Ⓐ Ⓑ Ⓒ Ⓓ
16 Ⓕ Ⓖ Ⓗ Ⓘ   36 Ⓕ Ⓖ Ⓗ Ⓘ
17 Ⓐ Ⓑ Ⓒ Ⓓ   37 Ⓐ Ⓑ Ⓒ Ⓓ
18 Ⓕ Ⓖ Ⓗ Ⓘ   38 Ⓕ Ⓖ Ⓗ Ⓘ
19 Ⓐ Ⓑ Ⓒ Ⓓ   39 Ⓐ Ⓑ Ⓒ Ⓓ
20 Ⓕ Ⓖ Ⓗ Ⓘ   40 Ⓕ Ⓖ Ⓗ Ⓘ